A NEW
AIR TRANSPORT POLICY
FOR THE
NORTH ATLANTIC

A NEW
AIR TRANSPORT
POLICY FOR THE
NORTH ATLANTIC

Saving an Endangered System

JESSE J. FRIEDMAN

FOREWORD BY ALAN S. BOYD

New York ATHENEUM 1976

DEDICATED

TO THE MEMORY OF

MY NOBLE FATHER AND MOTHER

Library of Congress Cataloging in Publication Data

FRIEDMAN, JESSE J
  A NEW AIR TRANSPORT POLICY FOR THE NORTH ATLANTIC.

  1. AERONAUTICS, COMMERCIAL—NORTH ATLANTIC OCEAN.
  2. AIR LINES—RATES. I. TITLE.
HE9777.F74 1976   387.7'1   76-15035
ISBN 0-689-10761-7

NOTE

BRITISH AIRWAYS and PAN AMERICAN WORLD AIRWAYS, in common with many other individuals and organizations, have become increasingly concerned about the economic position of airline operations on the North Atlantic routes. Traffic has been as high as 14 million passengers in a single year, but airline losses continue to mount. This "profitless growth syndrome" is not unique to these routes but the North Atlantic is of special importance to the airline industry because of the size and leading role of this market. Our fear is that today's Atlantic difficulties may be tomorrow's problems world wide.

Discussing these problems in the spring of last year, we agreed that some important new ideas had been put forward by Mr. Jesse J. Friedman, a well-known economic consultant to government and industry, in a 1973 study entitled "A Plan for Needed Regulation of Air Transport Service in the North Atlantic." We thought that these ideas deserved amplification and development and we therefore agreed that we would jointly commission Mr. Friedman to continue his studies and to make recommendations on the changes in the regulatory system necessary to overcome the commercial and financial problems of the North Atlantic.

This book is the outcome of Mr. Friedman's studies. It is a major intellectual contribution to the debate on international air transport regulation. We believe that the clarity of Mr. Friedman's analysis and the cogency of his arguments for change will commend themselves to a wide audience.

H. E. MARKING
Deputy Chairman and
  Managing Director
British Airways

WILLIAM T. SEAWELL
Chairman and
  Chief Executive Officer
Pan American World Airways

FOREWORD

"PROFITLESS BOOM" is a term that has been used to describe the situation of America's railroads. The term refers to the co-existence of growing volume and growing financial problems. The same phrase may well be applied to North Atlantic Civil Aviation carriers. It is the fact that despite more and more North Atlantic passengers, both scheduled and charter operations are suffering. The sickness continues and no remedy has so far worked.

The economic health of the North Atlantic air carriers of whatever type is essential if the public interest is to be saved. Inflation, stagflation, oil embargo, excess capacity, political unrest or government intrusion—there are enough villains to go around. But, we are short on constructive proposals to correct the problems, and the problems grow worse with each day that passes without solution.

Mr. Friedman has analyzed the existing situation with unusual accuracy and perception. His proposals are rational, balanced and insightful. They deserve the most thoughtful consideration—and consideration there must be!

The current situation cannot and will not continue. Change must occur and soon. The issue will either devolve into one of pure regulatory change, or change initiated by and developed primarily among the carriers involved. Regulation is reactive; it is constrained by law into rigidity. Far better for charter and scheduled airlines to develop concepts and mechanisms which can

be approved by regulators as being in the public interest than for the regulators, in the absence of airline
initiative, to be forced to design and impose change.

One question I believe readers should address: Will
the proposed change produce "healthy carriers and
adequate service?"

If the concepts espoused by Mr. Friedman can be
agreed upon, there remain enormous problems, though
not insurmountable, of definition and procedures—safeguards for the public and charter carriers as well as
scheduled carriers are essential and very difficult to
establish. But an effort must be made to correct the
present situation, and the Friedman Study points one
way to a constructive solution. It should mark the beginning of a most important dialogue from which must
come sane and workable North Atlantic Civil Aviation
Policy in the future. The debate must go on; it must
bring forth conclusions, for the situation on the North
Atlantic simply will not wait. If we fail to stabilize the
situation on the North Atlantic, the inevitable result
will be to undermine the entire system of world air
transport.

ALAN S. BOYD
Vice Chairman, Illinois Central Gulf Railroad

*Former Chairman, U.S. Civil Aeronautics Board,
and former U.S. Secretary of Transportation*

CONTENTS

A NEW
AIR TRANSPORT POLICY
FOR THE
NORTH ATLANTIC

I

Requisites of a Sound
Regulatory Policy

THE AIR LANES between North America
and Europe are the vital center of international
air transport. They account for 30 per cent of
all international air travel. Close to 13 million
passengers a year now rely—and, with the virtual
disappearance of marine passenger transport,
must rely—upon air transport to cross the North
Atlantic.[1] In a few short years, travel volume
will exceed 20 million passengers annually.

The North Atlantic lanes are not only the
most heavily traveled intercontinental passenger
routes in the world, they are also the most heavily supplied. As reported recently by the U.S.
Secretary of Transportation, there are now 30

[1] Detail in Appendix Table 1.

scheduled and 17 supplemental airlines operating in the North Atlantic.[2]

There is no question that the great North Atlantic air transport system is in sick condition. It has been so for some time. Losses are chronic and widespread, draining the financial resources of every segment of the industry, scheduled and supplemental, regardless of flag. For the North American and European airlines, which account for most of the traffic between the two continents, service across the North Atlantic is a large part of their global operations and, of necessity, heavily influences their financial performance as a whole.

The severe financial problems of the industry serving the North Atlantic require a basic change in the regulatory policy under which the industry now operates. The problems will not be cured by the natural course of events. Technological breakthroughs can not be looked to as a source of relief—there is nothing on the near horizon to compare with the dramatic productivity gains and cost reductions which accompanied the advent of the jets. Nor will traffic growth provide the answer. Clearly, it is not

[2] A Statement of National Transportation Policy by the Secretary of Transportation, September 17, 1975, Washington, D.C., p. 44.

lack of volume that has been responsible for the industry's ills. The red ink in the North Atlantic has flowed copiously despite a growth record equaled by few other industries. Over the 1963–73 decade, total air travel across the North Atlantic expanded at an average rate of more than 17 per cent a year.[3] Beginning in the late 'sixties the economic ills of the industry have become increasingly acute. A nine per cent sag in traffic in 1974, and a further, though less sharp, decline in 1975, aggravated the financial problems of the airlines. Even with this interruption in the long-term trend, air travel across the North Atlantic is currently about four and one-half times as great as in 1963. Few expect that growth rates, even when traffic recovers, can again be as high as in the past, and if high traffic volume has not heretofore been the means of achieving financial self-sufficiency in the North Atlantic it is not likely to be so in the future. The deep-lying economic problems which have plagued the North Atlantic service for years will remain and will continue to sap the vitality of the industry until they are cured.

Currently, North Atlantic passenger service operates with a gap between total revenues and

[3] Detail in Appendix Table 2.

total costs, including the cost of capital, of approximately $450 million annually.[4] Whether the deficiency is perceived as a failure to earn revenues sufficient to cover costs, or as an inability to contain costs within the level of revenues, or, more correctly, as the resultant of severe forces pressing simultaneously upon both revenues and costs, the recurring losses sustained in North Atlantic operations are symptomatic of a basic and serious economic malfunctioning of the air transport system serving that critically important area. Such a malfunction can not help but imperil the economic soundness of the system and, ultimately, the best economic interests of the public.

The public interest must suffer when the densest of all intercontinental passenger transport markets can not function on a self-sustaining basis. In the last analysis, the burden of supporting any essential public service rests, inescapably, upon the public, and the interest of the public is fulfilled only when the resources devoted to

[4] International Air Transport Association, Report of the Commercial Research Committee, June 1975, based upon data supplied by member carriers for the travel year 1974–5. Data cover scheduled North Atlantic passenger service only. Total loss for the year includes $125 million estimated requirement to cover equivalent of cost of equity capital. Losses in charter service, either for scheduled or supplemental carriers, are not included.

serving it and the terms on which that service is made available are in harmony with what the public using the service wants and needs and is prepared to pay for. Long-sustained unprofitability of operations in a major market is a sign both that efficient allocation of economic resources, which is crucial to a healthy world economy, is being frustrated, and that the cost of supporting the service is not being equitably borne by the various groups comprising the public.

It is possible for a time to finance chronically-losing services from profits earned elsewhere. But such internal subsidization merely shifts the burden of carrying the loss services to passengers in other areas and inevitably creates economic inefficiencies in both the subsidizing and the subsidized markets. And when long-continued losses must be financed through direct or indirect government subsidies, thus imposing the burden of the loss services upon the public at large, the effect is to create still another form of economic distortion.

If the economic troubles afflicting North Atlantic air service are to be successfully attacked, it is first necessary to realize that the answers are not to be found in simplistic explanations of the causes of the present situation.

A favorite explanation advanced by critics of the industry as the cause of its financial ills is that the large-scale purchases of wide-bodied jets in recent years were imprudent. In the North Atlantic as in other markets, rigidities introduced into flight scheduling by the quantum leap in aircraft size have undoubtedly complicated the industry's ability to deal with problems of surplus capacity. But quite apart from the futility of belaboring events which can not be undone, it is short-sighted to ignore the major operating economies, fuel savings, and reductions in airways and airport congestion—to say nothing of increased passenger comfort and convenience—which only the big jets have made possible.

Also one-sided is the inclination of the scheduled carriers and of the supplemental carriers to point the finger at each other's competitive actions and reactions as the main reason for the plight of the industry. The scheduled airlines tend to fix a generous portion of the blame for the unprofitability of their North Atlantic operations upon the rise of the supplemental airlines and the eroding effect of low-priced charter service upon scheduled traffic and yields. The supplemental airlines, in turn, attack the scheduled airlines for offering a vastly expanded share of scheduled services at discount-promotional fares regarded as unfairly and unreasonably close to charter fares.

It is true that the supplementals[5] have become a significant element in the structure of the North Atlantic air transport market—increasing their share of the market from 2 per cent to 16 per cent over the past 12 years—and that the financial performance of the scheduled airlines would probably have been better without the competition of the supplementals. Equally, the financial position of the supplementals would doubtless be better if, in serving the budget-conscious sectors of the travel market, they were shielded from the vigorous price and service competition of the scheduled carriers, which have offered various types of discount scheduled fares and substantially increased their own participation in the North Atlantic charter business. The scheduled carriers now account for about 40 per cent of the charter traffic.[6]

But a detached view suggests that both the rise of the supplementals with their planeload charter service and the competitive initiative and response of the scheduled airlines represent es-

[5] The term "supplemental airlines" or "charter airlines" is used in this study to refer to airlines operating charter service exclusively.

[6] Detail in Appendix Table 2.

sentially a reaction to the public's irrepressible demand for low-price travel. While the rivalry of scheduled and charter operators has taken a financial toll of both, it is important to keep in mind that the public, which every sector of public transportation exists to serve, has benefited from the expanded availability of low-price transportation which that rivalry has engendered in both scheduled and charter forms of service.

The ailing financial condition in the North Atlantic requires strong remedial measures—strong enough to revitalize the industry in a major way. But whatever changes are made in regulatory policy, the aim must be to preserve healthy competition between scheduled and supplemental carriers and to meet the needs of both. Scheduled and supplemental carriers not only coexist and compete in the same industry, they interact with, affect and are affected by, each other. Both have significant roles to play in the North Atlantic service system, and prudent regulatory policy must seek to accommodate the legitimate needs of both. This does not mean that each can be awarded its heart's desire. A proper balancing of the interests of contending parties on the basis of good public policy is part of the normal task of regulation. It is especially essential in devising a workable regulatory solution in the highly competitive environment of the North Atlantic.

The scheduled carrier and the supplemental carrier each possesses unique advantages. The scheduled carrier has the advantages associated with the ability to offer a broad product line ranging from the least-restricted, premium-commanding scheduled services, through the various discount-promotional scheduled categories carrying various degrees of travel restriction, to the charter service which is most restricted and, accordingly, lowest-priced. The supplemental carrier is a charter specialist, with all the benefits that go with operating at or near a full planeload basis. The scheduled carrier markets its seats at both retail and wholesale—selling its scheduled services direct to the traveler and, to a minor extent, on a group basis, and selling its charter services through wholesale channels. The supplemental is not only concentrated in charter operation but is a specialist in wholesale distribution. Both diversity and specialization offer production and marketing advantages, and diversified and specialized carriers alike have economic potentialities not available to the other in either the same form or degree. The job for regulators is to see that regulatory policies permit both types of carriers to take full advantage of their respective opportunities for efficient performance.

Maximizing economic efficiency is always a desirable objective for governments to pursue. It becomes an absolutely obligatory goal of regulatory policy when, as at present, the fires of inflation rage and to tolerate unnecessary waste borders on the unconscionable. Fostering the most efficient operation of air service is of vital concern to the public not only because of the stake of society in assuring efficient use of economic resources, but also because holding down the cost of the service is the only practical and reliable way to hold down its price. The central importance of promoting efficiency and minimizing costs is recognized in the 1970 International Air Transportation Policy of the United States, which declares for a system "based on the lowest cost of operating an efficient air transport system".[7]

For scheduled and supplemental airlines alike, costs in every category of airline expense have been surging upward, one wave of increase following hard upon another. Under the unremitting pressure of rising costs, fares for all types of services have irresistibly been swept higher

[7] Statement of International Air Transportation Policy of the United States, Approved by the President, June 22, 1970, p. 9.

and higher. The public is affected by higher fares in two ways: those who travel must pay more for their air passage, and those who can not afford to pay more do not travel. Under the stresses of inflation, increases in the prices paid for the human and material resources it takes to run an airline are unavoidable. To contain the impact of rising input prices upon fares and profits, the carriers have put into effect a variety of stringent cost-control measures. But major opportunities for cutting costs remain. Their realization requires, above all, a successful attack on the problem of excess and inadequately-utilized capacity which has long bedeviled the economics of North Atlantic air transport service. All the more because inflationary stresses are so severe, neither the industry nor its regulators can afford to ignore the significant cost reductions that more efficient employment of airline capacity, both scheduled and charter, could produce.

If economic self-sufficiency is to be attained in the North Atlantic, however, policy adjustments are indispensable in the revenue as well as in the cost column of the profit and loss ledger. The other side of the coin of maximizing efficiency is the establishment of a system of fares which provides the revenues needed to support an efficient air transport system, and which shares with the public the benefits of efficient operation. The entirety of these benefits belongs neither to the public nor to the airlines. Both have a proper claim. The principle for sharing the benefits of transport efficiency can be stated simply: fares should be no higher than the level needed to enable the airline system, under efficient operation, to cover its costs and sustain the capital investment required to meet diverse and growing public demands, and fares can go no lower than that level without compromising the economic soundness of the system and its ability to sustain the service.

The test of whether a fare level is too low is the sufficiency of revenues to meet the operating and capital costs of an efficient transport system, including an adequate profit. The test of whether a fare level is too high is whether the profit it produces under efficient operation is, by any reasonable standard, excessive.

The fare level at which the interests and needs of producers and consumers of air service are balanced is, in the crisp phrase of the Report of the Edwards Committee, "the minimum economic price which can be contrived"[8]—"mini-

---

[8] "British Air Transport in the Seventies", Report of the Committee of Inquiry into Civil Air Transport (Chairman, Sir Ronald Edwards), HMSO, London, 1969, p. 9.

mum" in this context expressing the entitlement of air travelers to the lowest prices which adequate and efficient service makes possible, and "economic" defining the financial ability of airlines to create and maintain such service. The object, as amplified by the U.K. Civil Aviation Act 1971, is to assure that air transport services "satisfy all substantial categories of demand . . . at the lowest level of charges consistent with a high standard of safety in operating the services and an economic return to efficient operators on the sums invested in providing the services. . .".[9] And the same object is at the heart of the U.S. Congressional declaration of policy in the Federal Aviation Act, mandating the Civil Aeronautics Board to "foster sound economic conditions" in air transportation and to promote "adequate, economical, and efficient service by air carriers at reasonable charges".[10]

Just as there is need to meet a range of demands, there is need for a range of fares to be applied. An economic level of fares thus refers not to a single fare, but a structure of different

[9] Section 3(1) of the Civil Aviation Act 1971, setting out the broad objectives of Government policy for the British civil air transport industry, as cited in "Civil Aviation Policy Guidance", Cmnd. 4899, HMSO, London, 1972, p. 1.

[10] Federal Aviation Act, 25 Stat. 980, 49 U.S.C. 402.

fares for different services, rationally related to each other and, in the aggregate, meeting the test of the minimum economic price that can be contrived—a composite fare level which is, as a thoughtful Civil Aviation Authority official has put it, "firmly rooted in the fundamental requirements of airline economics—which I sum up as the need to ensure that efficient airlines can remain viable".[11]

Clearly, the interest of the public is best advanced when the air service it needs in major established markets such as the North Atlantic is both efficiently organized and self-sustaining, and when the economic costs associated with efficient operation, including no more than a reasonable profit, are covered by the revenues collected. Clearly, the public interest is not well-served when efficient enterprises find themselves unable to cover the economic costs of the service they render.

Just as the satisfaction of all substantial categories of public demand at the lowest economic fares made possible by efficient operation should be the desired result of a soundly-functioning air transport system, it must be the ruling purpose of any sound regulatory policy. Theoretically,

[11] Ray Colegate, Address to Symposium on Mass Air Travel in Europe, Zurich, May 21/22, 1970, p. 13.

competition—the force that Richmond in his *Regulation and Competition in Air Transportation* has neatly termed "vying for economic advantage"[12]—could be relied upon to achieve approximately the same result. Competition, when functioning effectively, induces successful economic performance by promoting maximum production of goods and services in the widest range of both established and innovative forms at the lowest prices and in a manner which helps to assure the most productive use of economic wealth and the enhancement of economic welfare. The competitive struggle for the custom and favor of the public constitutes, in principle, the most effective pressure upon sellers to provide the most efficient means of supplying the public with the most of the best for the least— "a set of powerful motivations, stimulations, and drives toward increased output, product improvement, cost reduction: in general, towards increased efficiency in the use of resources".[13]

While the theoretical ideal of competition is

[12] Samuel B. Richmond, "Regulation and Competition in Air Transportation", Columbia University Press, New York, 1961, p. 21.

[13] Edward S. Mason, "The New Competition", in the Yale Review, Autumn 1953, as reprinted in his "Economic Concentration and the Monopoly Problem", Atheneum, New York, 1964, p. 375.

an invaluable tool of economic analysis, departures from that ideal are the common experience. In international air transportation particularly, the theoretical conditions required for the operation of perfect competition are not only conspicuously lacking but politically out of the question. Even in the United States, where an intense controversy rages over proposals to reduce regulatory control over rates and operating rights, the proponents of deregulation typically limit their proposals to domestic air transport, pointing out that the international scene poses unique problems. Thus, the recent Report of the CAB Special Staff on "Regulatory Reform", which recommends substantial deregulation in domestic service, observes that "the study has not focussed on international air transportation, where the institutional and legal framework is of an entirely different nature."[14] Senator Edward Kennedy of Massachusetts, the leading advocate in the United States Senate of substantial deregulation of domestic air transport, has stated that "international air transportation creates economic facts and circumstances which are basically different from those of the domestic industry, and it is not appropriate to automat-

[14] Report of the CAB Special Staff on Regulatory Reform, Civil Aeronautics Board, Washington, D.C., 1975, p. 17.

ically apply to the international field concepts of deregulation of rates and entry that are appropriate for the domestic industry."[15] As a stern academic critic of the international air transport industry has expressed it, "political considerations make a purely competitive environment an unfeasible alternative to the present industry structure and also render somewhat dubious the ability of competition to produce economically efficient performance."[16]

So long as the network of air routes and rights among sovereign nations remains, as in the past, dependent upon agreements between governments and inseparable from considerations of foreign economic policy and international prestige[17]—and that means for all of the foreseeable future—international air transport, including

---

[15] Letter from Senator Edward M. Kennedy to Jesse J. Friedman, December 8, 1975.

[16] Mahlon R. Straszheim, "The International Airline Industry", Brookings Institution, Washington, D.C., 1969, p. 202.

[17] "[G]overnments are willing to forego other investments, to tax their citizens, and to commit their political capital to develop civil aviation. In some countries, civil aviation even becomes part of the reigning mythology—an indispensable part of the national character, something to be given high priority among their commercial and economic interests." Raymond J. Waldman, U.S. Deputy Assistant Secretary of State for Transportation and Telecommunications, Address to International Aviation Club, Washington, D.C., February 18, 1975, p. 3.

service in the North Atlantic, must be governed by a policy of controlled competition. The question for the regulator is always how much control and how much competition comprise the right blend, and the answer is never easy. Finding the most effective combination of control and competition poses a more difficult challenge to the regulatory art than adopting either drastically rigid control or totally unrestricted competition, even if those extreme alternatives were available.

The right mixture of control and competition for regulators to compound must in the end be determined by the conditions they seek to achieve. If a well-functioning North Atlantic service performing in the public interest is epitomized by the ability of airlines to meet the range of public demands efficiently and at lowest economic fares, it follows that a sound regulatory policy for the North Atlantic requires the kind and extent of control and the kind and extent of competition which, in tandem, will best contribute to achievement of optimum efficiency and establishment of a rational structure of fares at as low a level as that efficiency makes possible.

It is healthy for regulators to hold a presumption, even a strong presumption, in favor of competition. But a presumption is not a commandment. To the extent that competition is politically feasible and can be economically effective in achieving the all-important objectives of maximum efficiency and lowest economic price, it is sound for competition to prevail over control. To the extent, however, that competition is ruled out politically, or in practice, would, because of the economic environment of the North Atlantic, thwart rather than fulfill the basic objectives of maximum efficiency and economic price, some type of control must be placed on competition—but always with those same objectives paramount.

Political realism in this context does not require accepting the lowest common denominator of reigning government attitudes as a fixed template of policy. As is always the case when nations must agree upon a common course to meet an unavoidable problem, there is room for reason, for good sense, for persuasion, for enlightened self-interest, for negotiation, to be brought into play. The borders of the politically possible can be stretched by these influences. Politics is the art of the pragmatic, and in the skillful practice of that art the most serious fault is rigidity. Times change, problems change. When wisdom prevails, even long-established policies must give way as unprecedented opportunities are presented or unprecedented dangers loom. But

II

Achieving Improved
Efficiency

THERE IS no more universally accepted goal
of economic systems than the attainment of
economic efficiency.[1] The premium which modern economists attach to that goal is evident
throughout the enormous literature of the economics of welfare, a subject which has become
practically synonymous with the economics of
efficiency.[2] Many economic thinkers, from the
Italian economist, Enrico Barone, writing early

[1] See Heinz Kohler, "Welfare Planning: An Analysis
of Capitalism Versus Socialism", Wiley, New York, 1966,
pp. 4–7.
[2] Kalman J. Cohen and Richard M. Cyert, "Theory of
the Firm: Resource Allocation in a Market Economy",
Prentice-Hall, Englewood Cliffs, N.J., 1965, p. 299. See
also E. J. Mishan, "Welfare Economics", 2nd ed., Random
House, New York, 1969.

in the century, to Tjalling Koopmans, Nobel Laureate in Economics, have held that the efficiency optimum held out by economic theory is applicable either in a competitive economic system or in a system wholly devoid of competition.[3]

Regardless of theoretical concepts, it is clear that the goal of economic efficiency can never be perfectly attained, that the textbook conditions for optimal economic results are found nowhere on earth, neither in a controlled nor a

[3] Enrico Barone, "The Ministry of Production in the Collectivist State", in Friedrich von Hayek, ed., "Collectivist Economic Planning", Routledge, London, 1935, pp. 245–90. Tjalling C. Koopmans, "Efficient Allocation of Resources", in Econometrica, October 1951, pp. 455–65.

See also Oskar Lange, "On the Economic Theory of Socialism", University of Minnesota Press, 1938, reprinted by McGraw-Hill, New York, 1965. "The rules of consistency of decisions and of efficiency in carrying them out in a socialist economy are exactly the same as those that govern the actual behavior of entrepreneurs in a purely competitive market. Competition forces entrepreneurs to act much as they would have to act were they managers of production in a socialist system." Lange, p. 98.

For the view of some economists that efficiency optimization is not achievable under the centralized direction of a socialist economy, see Ludwig von Mises, "Economic Calculation in the Socialist Commonwealth", reprinted in von Hayek, op. cit., chapter III; Lionel Robbins, "The Great Depression", Macmillan, London, 1934; and Friedrich von Hayek, "Socialist Calculation: The Competitive Solution", in Economica, May 1940.

market economy. Efficient use of resources is nevertheless of vital importance to successful economic performance and the well-being of peoples. It is therefore the business of governments to strive to bring about, as nearly as possible, the economic efficiency that would be achieved under ideal arrangements.[4]

Governments move in that direction whenever regulatory power is used in a way that enables enterprises, whether privately or publicly owned, to perform more efficiently. Efficient performance of an enterprise is, at bottom, a matter of ends and means, of "ends produced" in relation to "means used", of output per unit of input.[5] It is, in common parlance, a matter of cost of production.

In air transport, as in other industries, efficiency equates with the minimization of cost. "Minimizing the production cost of the airline service, whatever its quality, is a necessary condition for economic efficiency . . . Efficiency in the provision of airline service requires . . . that services of given quality be produced at lowest feasible cost . . .", Douglas and Miller

[4] "Efficiency in the allocation of resources calls for policies to mitigate the inadequacies of an imperfect market structure." D. M. Winch, "Analytical Welfare Economics", Penguin, London, 1971, p. 198.

[5] Kenneth M. Boulding, "Economic Analysis", 3rd ed., Harper, New York, 1955, p. 717.

emphasize in their recent *Economic Regulation of Domestic Air Transport.*[6]

Failure to observe these basic, almost axiomatic, principles of maximizing efficiency and minimizing cost is responsible in a large way for the economic troubles experienced for so long in the North Atlantic. Heavy investment in fleet replacement and expansion with the most modern and sophisticated flight equipment which advanced technology can provide has made the airlines increasingly capital-intensive. At the same time, capital has become extremely costly. The combination of heightened capital intensity and capital cost makes it imperative that the airlines use their investment capital to best advantage. Yet the North Atlantic air transport system operates year after year with an appalling inefficiency of capacity use. That inefficiency takes two forms: the amount of capacity operated is far greater than the public demands or requires, and the capacity operated is inadequately utilized.

The waste of capacity in the North Atlantic is a waste of costly resources: capital, labor, fuel, and other resources as well. Such waste is intolerable for the airlines and a disservice to the

[6] George W. Douglas and James C. Miller, III, "Economic Regulation of Domestic Air Transport: Theory and Policy", Brookings Institution, Washington, D.C., 1974, pp. 62, 72.

public's twin interest in optimizing the use of economic resources and holding down the expense of travel. That the waste has been permitted to continue, while costs soar and deficits accumulate, suggests a defect of industry initiative or of regulatory leadership or both. It can not be allowed to go on if the industry is to be restored to economic soundness and financial health.

The inefficiency of capacity use in the North Atlantic, and the potential that exists for major cost savings through more efficient use, are illustrated by the fact that, on the average, North Atlantic scheduled service operates with little more than half its seats filled. Sir Anthony Milward, then Chairman of British European Airways, remarked a number of years ago that the proportion of capacity that is sold reflects not only the efficiency, but the inefficiency, of airline operation. "Load factor does not merely indicate how much of one's product is being consumed in any given period; it also reveals how much of that product is being thrown away."[7]

The notion of inefficiency always "implies

[7] Anthony H. Milward, "Wasted Seats in Air Transport: An Examination of the Importance of Load Factor", Brancker Memorial Lecture, February 14, 1966, as reprinted in Institute of Transport Journal, May 1966, p. 347.

that an available superior course of action that *might* have been taken was ignored".[8] In the North Atlantic, the available, superior course of action that could significantly increase efficiency involves, in a nutshell, making more economic use of equipment. The shortest and surest route to increased efficiency involves controlling and integrating scheduled and charter capacity. The discussion that follows is concerned with an examination of why this approach is desirable and how it could contribute to increased efficiency of capacity use, and thus to lowered costs and improved financial results, in the North Atlantic.

Controlling Scheduled Capacity

Excess capacity in North Atlantic scheduled air transport is different in marked degree from the problem as it is found in other airline markets and different in basic form from excess capacity as it is experienced in most other industries.[9]

[8] Israel M. Kirzner, "Competition and Entrepreneurship", University of Chicago Press, Chicago and London, 1973, p. 235.

[9] "The term 'excess capacity' . . . has a dangerously deceptive appearance of simplicity and definiteness. As a

As the term in normally used in the general run of industry, excess capacity refers to the difference between the supply a productive unit is capable of producing over some period and the supply it actually produces in response to demand. The concept is different in a business devoted to producing scheduled air services, where the unit of capacity is the flight. While the supply of seats that a scheduled North Atlantic flight is capable of producing over some period will exceed actual demand (the difference being mirrored by the average load factor), that supply never exceeds—and in fact is identical with—the supply it actually produces. A factory produces supply at the level of demand, but a flight produces supply at the level of capacity.[10]

A certain amount of "slack" capacity is not only normal but mandatory if a scheduled system is to provide good service. What is generally

---

matter of fact, although the basic idea of the concept is clearly enough suggested by the term, the variety of particular meanings that may be attached to it is so great that unless it is used and interpreted with the greatest of care, it is likely to result in serious confusion of thought." John M. Cassels, "Excess Capacity and Monopolistic Competition", in Quarterly Journal of Economics, May 1937, p. 426.

[10] A factory can also produce for inventory, while the product of a flight is non-storable.

meant by excess capacity in scheduled air transport is the "excessive" slackness of the capacity being offered in a market over the supply that can be sold at an acceptable degree of profit. Although both seats and flights are relevant in measuring the amount of capacity, or supply, excess capacity is best described in terms of the surplus frequencies offered beyond those needed to meet public demand satisfactorily and sustain a profitable level of operation.

Students of airline economics have given increasing attention in recent years to the basic importance of capacity competition in the generation of excess capacity in scheduled air service.[11] There is general agreement that the fre-

[11] See: George C. Eads, "Competition in the Domestic Trunkline Industry: Too Much or Too Little", in Almarin Phillips, ed., "Promoting Competition in Regulated Markets", Brookings Institution, Washington, D.C., 1975; Robert W. Simpson, "A Theory for Domestic Airline Economics", in Proceedings, Fifteenth Annual Meeting, Transportation Research Forum, Chicago, 1974, pp. 295–308; George W. Douglas and James C. Miller, III, "Quality Competition, Industry Equilibrium, and Efficiency in the Price-Constrained Airline Market", in American Economic Review, September 1974, pp. 657–669; Walter Gelerman and Richard de Neufville, "Planning for Satellite Airports", in Transportation Engineering Journal, August 1973, pp. 537–551; Herbert B. Hubbard and William G. Williamson, "The Effect of Competition in Air Transportation, presented at Twelfth Annual Symposium of AGIFORS, Nathanya, Israel, October 1972; William

quency of flight availability is an important aspect of quality competition among airlines, that excess capacity in scheduled air transport arises particularly from the role of frequencies in the competitive struggle of rival airlines to hold or increase market share, and that the intensity of frequency competition is greatest when the number of competing carriers in the market is greatest.

A change in a carrier's share of the total capacity—more specifically, of the total flight fre-

E. Fruhan, Jr., "The Fight for Competitive Advantage", Division of Research, Harvard Graduate School of Business Administration, Boston, 1972; Alfred E. Kahn, "The Economics of Regulation", Vol. 2, Wiley, New York, 1972, pp. 211–212; Joseph V. Yance, "The Possibility of Loss-Producing Equilibrium in Air Carrier Markets", Boston University, Department of Economics, Boston, 1971; Gilles Renard, "Competition in Air Transportation: An Econometric Approach", M.S. Thesis, Massachusetts Institute of Technology, Cambridge, 1970; Arthur De-Vany, "The Economics of Quality Competition: Theory and Evidence on Airline Flight Scheduling", Department of Economics, University of California, Los Angeles, 1969; N.K. Taneja, "Airline Competition Analysis", Massachusetts Institute of Technology, Flight Transportation Laboratory, Cambridge, 1968; Roland E. Miller, "Domestic Airline Efficiency: An Application of Linear Programming", M.I.T. Press, Cambridge, 1963. For an earlier reference to the problems of competition by capacity, see Jesse J. and Murray N. Friedman, "The New Economics of the Airline Industry", in Public Utilities Fortnightly, August 17, 1961.

quencies—offered in a market closely affects its share of that market. (Where the aircraft types employed by competing carriers in a market have similar seating capacity, of course, capacity share will be the same on the basis of either frequencies or seats.) The influence of various factors on the correlation between frequency share and market share has yet to be established with precision, but the strong positive relationship between the two is beyond dispute. As stated in a recent study for the National Productivity Commission in the United States, "the most powerful force in determining the market share is simply the relative number of flights offered by each competitor".[12] The more airlines vying for the traffic in a market, the stronger the incentive for frequency competition. "[M]arket share increases with frequency share. The higher the number of competitors, the faster the increase."[13] And the more vigorously those airlines compete, the more excess capacity they create. "The greater the tendency

[12] George W. Douglas, "Productivity in the Domestic Airline Industry", National Productivity Commission, Washington, D.C., 1975, p. 8.

[13] Renard, op. cit., p. 33. See also Eads, op. cit., pp. 26–27, and George W. Douglas, "Excess Capacity, Service Quality and the Structure of Airline Fares", in Proceedings, Transportation Research Forum, Chicago, 1971.

of firms to act competitively . . . the greater will be the availability of seats and the lower their load factors."[14]

Several investigators have concluded that the relationship between capacity share and market share, when plotted on a graph, typically takes the form of an "S"-shaped curve, meaning that, beyond a threshold level, increases in capacity share are accompanied by more than proportionate market gains while decreases in capacity share are accompanied by more than proportionate market losses. Such a relationship implies that "a carrier who 'stands pat' in the face of competitive capacity additions does not merely fail to expand his profit base as might be the case in many industries . . . [but] will rapidly find himself losing both profit and passengers on an absolute basis".[15] Equally, the relationship implies the reverse, that a carrier unilaterally initiating a capacity reduction in a market or matching a reduction initiated by a competitor will be worse off than by standing pat.

The acid test for an individual carrier weigh-

[14] Lawrence J. White, "Quality, Competition and Regulation: Evidence from the Airline Industry", in Richard E. Caves and Marc J. Roberts, eds., "Regulating the Product: Quality and Variety", Ballinger, Cambridge, Mass., 1975, p. 25.
[15] Fruhan, op. cit., p. 129.

ing a decision to reduce the number of flights operated is whether the out-of-pocket expenses saved exceed the revenues lost. Even if the market gains or losses in prospect are not quite as pronounced as the S-relationship would suggest, the marginal revenues and costs associated with adding or subtracting flights can produce a situation in which an individual carrier will find it financially more advantageous (or less disadvantageous) to match the frequency increases of competitors—and to refrain from matching their frequency decreases—than not to do so. Each carrier following such a course in faithful pursuit of its economic self-interest contributes to a market-wide buildup of excess capacity— with its concomitants of reduced load factors, increased costs, and erosion of profits for all. This process will be more marked as the number of competing carriers in the market increases and the vying for competitive advantage becomes more intense. The 30 scheduled airlines operating in the North Atlantic market make that market by far the most competitive in the world.[16] It is not surprising, then, that the problem of excess capacity, with all its attendant dis-

[16] Notwithstanding that not all the carriers serve all of the submarkets of the North Atlantic, and some of the carriers are of relatively minor importance.

abilities, appears there in its most extreme form.

Experience shows that it is vain to hope that the problem of excess capacity in the North Atlantic can be solved by the unilateral actions of individual carriers. Unilateral reductions of capacity on any substantial scale are unlikely because of the economic damage which any individual carrier undertaking such reductions could expect to incur if its competitors did not follow suit. By abstaining from matching a capacity reduction, competitors can gain at the expense of the initiator. By matching a reduction, they forego that advantage. And if no capacity reduction at all is initiated, all suffer.

Some analysts have suggested that airlines should be more rational than to follow individual commercial strategies which, in the aggregate, are bound to perpetuate, if not aggravate, the evils attendant upon excess capacity. But without some assurance that capacity reductions will in fact be matched by competitors, the reluctance of airlines to initiate such reductions is not only understandable, it is a sheer matter of self-defense. To expect airlines to be so "enlightened" as to surrender market share to rivals, who need only react in a less enlightened fashion to aggrandize their position at the expense of the market share and profitability of the presumably unbenighted carrier, is asking for entrepreneurial behavior which is alien to every commercial instinct.

Such behavior would also be contrary to the ordinary dictates of vigorous competition. In a competitive environment, keen rivalry decrees that firms strive for market share in the interest of maximizing their profits (or limiting their losses). Not every advance in a market is profitable, and not every retreat is unprofitable. But profit or loss in this context is determined at the margin. The deletion of one flight does not permit proportionate reductions in expenses related to various support and overhead functions. Thus, the load factor needed to cover incremental expenses associated with a single flight can be 15 to 25 percentage points lower than that needed to cover fully allocated costs.[17] There are isolated instances of markets, including some in the North Atlantic, where losses have mounted so intolerably high that an individual scheduled airline has found itself with no practical alternative but to take unilateral action to reduce frequencies or withdraw en-

[17] Talk by Melvin A. Brenner, Vice President, Marketing Planning, Trans World Airlines, at the Aviation and Space Writers Luncheon, Washington, D.C., January 15, 1975, p. 10.

tirely from the market. But as a general matter it will not be realistic to look for individual unilateral action to bring about any substantial industry-wide reduction of scheduled capacity in the North Atlantic so long as market share is clearly and intimately tied to the frequency of flight offerings, so long as a unilateral cutback of frequencies costs more in revenues than it saves in out-of-pocket expenses, and so long as competitors have a profit incentive to seize the share of the market given up and are free to do so. And the more competitors in the market and the more vigorous the rivalry for business, the greater will be the deterrent to individual action to reduce capacity.

The factors deterring unilateral reduction of capacity in the North Atlantic are reinforced by the relatively low frequency of service by individual carriers. On many city-pair routes in the North Atlantic, for example, frequency cuts mean dropping to less-than-daily service and would down-grade the scheduling image of an airline in relation to a competitor continuing to offer daily service.

If the objective is to improve load factors and bring down costs in the North Atlantic by squeezing out of the market a significant portion of the excess capacity which now depresses financial results, reliance on spontaneous individual action will not suffice. A more forthright approach is needed than the wishful thinking that the commercial and competitive incentives customary and appropriate to an individual business strategy will be suspended by an individual airline on the prospect of beneficial results which only a common strategy can produce. The only effective way to reduce excess capacity in the North Atlantic is by forthright multilateral limitation, using the device of reciprocal capacity reduction agreements made subject to regulatory approval. If capacity reductions are mutually undertaken, the risk of ceding market position to a competitor is overcome, the temptation to take unfair advantage of the unilateral action of a competitor is eliminated, and all carriers benefit.

The public also benefits in that the cost saving which accompanies reduction in the number of flights makes it possible to hold fares below levels that would otherwise be necessary.

It is essential to make sure, however, that the public is not at the same time disadvantaged by impairment of the quality of air service at its disposal. If the number of flights offered by the carriers is too drastically reduced under a capacity limitation arrangement, one of the basic quality characteristics of scheduled service—ability to book on short notice—may be undermined. Even when average load factors are inordinately low because of clearly excessive capacity, there will be times, particularly during the heavy travel periods, when individual flights are fully booked and a passenger will be unable to obtain a seat on a preferred flight. As average load factors increase, the chances of such unavailability will rise. The purpose of capacity limitation is to lower costs by reducing the number of flights which must be operated. Carrying essentially the same volume of traffic on fewer flights means both higher load factors and a reduction in the flight choices available to passengers. A balance must therefore be struck between the need to minimize airline costs and the need of the public for adequate scheduled service. It would be a function of government regulators, before giving approval to capacity limitation arrangements in the North Atlantic, to make sure that a proper balance of this kind is maintained.

Theoretically, *any* reduction in flight frequencies is tantamount to *some* reduction in the quality of service. Regulators need not be concerned with such hair-splitting, however. The convenience of the public is an important consideration, but minor reductions in convenience can not be permitted to carry decisive weight. The airline industry, in the North Atlantic as elsewhere, is sometimes criticized for what is alleged to be an inordinate propensity to compete by means of flight frequencies. The inference is that, but for this inclination, fewer frequencies would be operated and excess capacity would be prevented. Similarly, objections to capacity limitation agreements are sometimes raised on the ground that it would be preferable to reduce frequencies by individual, rather than concerted, action. But whether reduced frequencies are achieved by unilateral or multilateral decision, or by not increasing frequencies in the first place, the implications for public convenience and the quality of service are exactly the same. The task for regulators is to make it possible for the airlines to place scheduled service in the North Atlantic on a self-sustaining basis without sacrificing the essential character of such service. While no precise mathematical rule can be established, the amount of capacity operated at present in the North Atlantic is so manifestly and abundantly excessive in relation to the number of seats sold that it should be possible to bring about a major reduction in flight frequencies without significant inconvenience to the traveling public.

Advocates of a "free market" approach to

the economic problems of air transportation argue that the best cure for excess capacity is to let it cure itself through unrestricted competition, regardless of the financial hardships, business failures, and other upheavals that may be entailed before an "equilibrium" is achieved, and that for best results unrestrained price rivalry should be accompanied by freedom of entry. As a solution to the problems of the North Atlantic, where chronic losses have already produced considerable financial suffering, such Spartan counsel—even if the beneficial results theoretically flowing from it could be guaranteed—is unlikely to generate enthusiasm among the governments concerned. Politics aside, moreover, such a course in the North Atlantic has little to recommend it from a public-interest standpoint.

In his *Market Structure, Organization and Performance*, Professor Almarin Phillips of the University of Virginia has questioned whether, in industry generally, there is any evidence that trying to eliminate excess capacity through the mechanism of unrestrained rivalry serves the public interest. He states:

"Performance does depend on the degree of rivalry among firms. Performance is not, however, monotonically related to rivalry . . . [B]ecause of the interdependent nature of rivalry, continuously increasing it does not produce continuous improvements in performance. An equilibrium similar to that of pure competition does not emerge; instead, beyond some point performance tends to deteriorate from excessive rivalry and market chaos.

". . . The performance of excess rivalry suggests that neither the social interest nor the private interest is being adequately served . . . Excess rivalry is often associated with excess capacity, with new firms replacing those that fail, secularly low—even negative—profits, and a lack of technological change . . . [A]t one extreme of rivalry neither the public nor the private interest is rewarded."[18]

In the case of North Atlantic air transport, where scheduled air fares are established by industry agreement, subject to regulatory review, price rivalry is restricted but government authority operates to insure that rates are reasonable. While government regulatory agencies do not prescribe the level of fares—and can not feasibly do so because in international markets they lack exclusive jurisdiction—their review power is nevertheless substantial and no rate deemed unreasonable may be put into effect.

Entry is also restricted. As in the case of fares,

[18] Almarin Phillips, "Market Structure, Organization and Performance", Harvard University Press, Cambridge, Mass., 1962, pp. 36–39.

no single government has exclusive control over an international route authorization. North Atlantic air transport, however, does not suffer from a shortage of competitors but from a surfeit of them, numbering 47 scheduled and charter carriers by recent count. No other airline market in the world approaches the North Atlantic with respect to density of competition. It is difficult, therefore, to consider entry limitations a factor of any consequence in accounting for excess capacity.

In considering remedies of the free-market type for the vexing problem of excess capacity in the North Atlantic, it is essential to beware of adverse side effects. Some critics of capacity reduction agreements in the North Atlantic[19] argue that the scheduling rivalry which generates excess capacity is directly related to the prevailing level of fares, that the presence of excess capacity in a market indicates that prices are too high, and that the number of frequencies operated would be reduced, load factors increased, and excess capacity mitigated, if fares were lowered, preferably by removing all restraints on price rivalry. This argument rests

[19] See for example, George W. Douglas, "Excess Capacity and Fares in Transatlantic Air Transport", Proceedings of International Conference on Transportation Research (Bruges, 1973), Chicago, 1974, pp. 262–267.

ultimately on the premise that if only marginal revenues are made sufficiently unattractive the airlines will be motivated to reduce the number of flights they operate and load factors will increase. It is certainly conceivable that a reduction in fares could, by raising the marginal break-even load factor, make it uneconomic to operate many of the flights now operated. Serious as the burden which excess capacity places upon operating costs undoubtedly is, however, curing the problem by creating a more serious problem is not the answer. Even a substantial reduction in costs would be futile if it were achieved through a still greater reduction in revenues. The real challenge to the airlines and to regulators is not merely to cure excess capacity, but to do so in a way that does not aggravate the present situation of financial distress.

With losses already so high in the North Atlantic and costs steadily mounting, fare reductions can be justified only if the loss in unit revenues is more than offset by beneficial effects of increased passenger volume and higher load factors. Proponents of major fare reduction as the solution to excess capacity can offer no assurance that the net effect of such fare reductions on airline profits would be positive. Price reduction is not a magic catalyst that unfailingly transmutes airline distress into airline prosperity. Pricing policy is one of the most difficult aspects of airline marketing. It involves highly elusive and unsettled questions of the sensitivity of demand to different fare levels. Whether a particular reduction will have positive or negative effects upon industry profitability depends upon complicated and interdependent demand and cost functions. Except where political pressures have brought about distortions in specific markets, the present fare level presumably reflects the judgment of airline managements as to the trade-off between the possibilities of increased traffic and the certainties of reduced yields, and reflects also their conclusion that at any lower fare level airline profits would be lower, not higher, than at present. That judgment can be wrong. But it is not proved so by an easy assumption that if only fares are lowered all will be for the best.

Given the great uncertainties about the price elasticities of air transport demand under varying conditions, and the acknowledged fundamental differences between international air transport and the goods market models of classical economics, it requires an extraordinary degree of faith in the universal curative powers of the free market solution to economic problems to accept, on the strength of little more than dogma, that the North Atlantic air transport system can not only be purged of excess capacity but restored to financial health simply by removing all regulatory checks upon price rivalry or by establishing prices close to the level that such rivalry would produce.

Consumers naturally prefer lower prices to higher. But, despite the seeming paradox, not all price reductions are good for the public.

First of all, as a leading advocate of the free-market approach concedes, one of the by-products of unrestrained price rivalry in the North Atlantic would be the disappearance of direct scheduled services to all points other than the main gateways. For example, all existing nonstop scheduled service between Europe and inland U.S. cities would become extinct and additional services now under consideration would be foreclosed.[20]

[20] Douglas, "Excess Capacity and Fares in Transatlantic Air Transport", op. cit., p. 267. Douglas does not regard the total disappearance of direct transatlantic service to inland U.S. cities as an economic loss. "We would anticipate . . . that some direct scheduled services would disappear. The economy fare scheduled services would be viable only in the principal gateway markets, where the traffic density is adequate. In the secondary markets, such as service from an inland U.S. city to a principal European gateway, most travellers will find it cheaper to travel

Furthermore, a claim of soundness from a public-interest standpoint can only be made for price reductions which are consistent with operating on an economic basis. The public-interest objective of a minimum economic price means not only a *minimum* price but, equally, an *economic* price. Virtually all economists agree that minimizing prices is best achieved—in fact, can only be achieved—by minimizing costs. The case for capacity reduction agreements is founded on the same objective: lower fares through lower costs. The basic difference between the free-market and capacity-agreement approaches to that objective is in their starting points. The free-market advocates would start with lower prices, with the aim of inducing a contraction of capacity, thus raising load factors and reducing costs, thereby justifying the price reductions. The capacity-agreements approach focuses on the reduction of excess capacity as the first step, using capacity limitation to raise load factors and reduce costs, thus providing the key requisite to holding down or bringing down

---

via the principal U.S. gateway cities, exploiting the economy fares in the transatlantic segment. The demise of direct service in these markets, by definition, however, does not result in a welfare loss to those travellers. Rather, we would interpret the current existence of these services as an artifact of the inefficient cartel equilibrium."

fares. The free-market approach is necessarily built on the faith that price reduction will eventually produce its own cost-reducing vindication. The capacity-agreements approach is more pragmatic in that it would achieve a cost reduction before reflecting it in the price level.

If airline earnings in the North Atlantic were lush, the argument for experimentation along the free-market line might have more appeal. At a time when the airlines are unable, by several hundred million dollars a year, to cover their operating and capital costs, the capacity-limitation approach has the better claim to regulatory favor as the prudent line of action.

Capacity limitation agreements have been criticized by some as "anti-competitive". One of the most vociferous critics of capacity agreements on this ground has been the U.S. Department of Justice, which "has opposed, and continues to oppose, capacity reduction agreements, because they eliminate cariers' individual incentives to offer schedules best suited to the public's needs".[21]

The Department of Justice argues that ". . . capacity agreements reduce the output of

[21] Comments of the United States Department of Justice on Application of Pan American World Airways for emergency authorization of carrier discussions, April 2, 1974, Civil Aeronautics Board Docket 26516, p. 12.

competing airlines and therefore degrade the quality of service received by the public . . . [S]uch agreements disrupt the free play of market forces . . . Frequency of service is indisputably the paramount competitive device available to airline managements . . . Agreements that restrict capacity strike at the heart of the competitive air transportation system". The Justice Department would rely upon unilateral airline actions, induced by rate regulation, to bring down the level of unused capacity.[22]

There are two types of inconsistency in this line of thinking. While deploring the frequency-reducing purpose of agreements to limit capacity on the ground that such limitations impair the quality of air services, the Justice Department nevertheless favors another—and less reliable—means to accomplish the same purpose. Yet, regardless of how achieved, reductions of capacity have the same effect upon service. Secondly, while it objects to capacity agreements on the ground that the reduction of frequencies is arrived at in concert, the Justice Department is apparently quite willing to see the

[22] Brief of the United States Department of Justice to the Civil Aeronautics Board, February 7, 1975, Capacity Reduction Agreements Case, Docket 22908, pp. 1, 11–12, 53.

same result achieved through unilateral actions undertaken in the expectation that they will be parallelled by the unilateral actions of others. The U.S. antitrust agencies have in the past attacked such "concerted parallel action" in other industries as being tantamount to an overt agreement.

On this aspect of how best to bring about needed reductions in excess capacity, the Justice philosophy has been expounded as folows: "[I]f the carriers serving a market found themselves in a position where all were losing money, each would be likely to be able to identify flights which could be eliminated with a loss of relatively few passengers. Cutting these flights would serve not only to raise the carrier's average load factor in the market but would also serve as a signal to rivals of its willingness to engage in a 'mutual withdrawal'."[23] But if "mutual withdrawal" of frequencies by means of "signaling" among rivals is considered appropriate, it is difficult to understand why—aside from

[23] Direct testimony of the United States Department of Justice, April 26, 1974, Capacity Reduction Agreements Case, Docket 22908, p. 14. See also George Eads, "Airline Capacity Limitation Controls: Public Vice or Public Virtue", Proceedings, American Economic Association, May 1974, p. 368.

doctrinaire preoccupation with mere form—the same mutual withdrawal by means of forthright agreement is not.

In the United States, the arguments against capacity agreements have heretofore focussed primarily on their use in domestic U.S. air service. The case for capacity agreements is generally regarded as stronger in international markets. In its July 1975 order withdrawing approval of capacity reduction agreements in the four major transcontinental U.S. markets in which they had been in effect since 1971, the Civil Aeronautics Board, noting "the often decisively different circumstances", pointed out that "international capacity agreements may well continue to be acceptable even where a parallel domestic agreement would not be".[24]

In the past two years, several international capacity agreements have received CAB blessing. The impetus for these agreements came largely from the world fuel crisis which arose in October 1973. Until that time, while capacity arrangements were, and still are, commonly employed in international air services elsewhere, they were, as a matter of policy, rarely if ever

[24] U.S. Civil Aeronautics Board, Order 75-7-98, Capacity Reduction Agreements Case, decided July 21, 1975, p. 15.

approved on routes to and from the United States.

In November 1974 the Board approved capacity agreements involving scheduled services offered by U.S. and British carriers between London and various American cities;[25] by U.S. and Italian carriers between Rome and Milan and various American cities;[26] and by U.S. and Greek carriers in the New York–Athens market.[27] In each of these situations, the CAB found in its order that "mutual reductions in international capacity, when carefully monitored by the Board, can help to provide the public with optimum service in the face of the constraints imposed by the international fuel situation".

In December 1974, an agreement to limit capacity operated in the United States–Venezuela market was endorsed by the Board for the same reason.[28] An extension of that agreement is currently under CAB consideration.

[25] U.S. Civil Aeronautics Board, Order 74-2-93, February 22, 1974, covering service through March 1974; and Order 74-10-6, October 2, 1974, and Order 74-11-34, November 7, 1974, both covering service through April 1975.

[26] U.S. Civil Aeronautics Board, Order 74-11-52, November 12, 1974, covering service through March 1975.

[27] U.S. Civil Aeronautics Board, Order 74-11-54, November 13, 1974, covering service through March 1975.

[28] U.S. Civil Aeronautics Board, Order 74-12-1, December 2, 1974.

In March 1975, the Board approved a capacity-limitation agreement governing scheduled service between the United States and Switzerland, stating: ". . . [R]ecognizing the special circumstances applicable with respect to both excess capacity and the financial losses of the U.S.-flag carriers in the transatlantic markets, and the responsibility of the Board, in accordance with the national program for fuel conservation, to consider measures which will avoid superfluous or extravagant utilization of fuel supplies, we have decided to approve the subject capacity agreement."[29]

In July 1975, the Board approved a capacity reduction agreement involving scheduled service between the U.S. and Australia, stating that the imposition of capacity restraints is justified because of the competitive environment and in the interest of curtailing excessive fuel usage. The Board added that the lack of load-factor standards of rate control—such as those adopted by the Board in reviewing domestic fares—works against the likelihood that unilateral restraint among competing international carriers to gear capacity to demand could be effective.[30]

[29] U.S. Civil Aeronautics Board, Order 75-3-67, March 21, 1975, covering service through October 1975.

[30] U.S. Civil Aeronautics Board, Order 75-7-27, July 3, 1975, covering service through October 1975.

In October 1975 the Board, in approving a U.S.-U.K. capacity agreement for the 1975–76 winter season covering service between London and New York, Chicago, Washington, and Boston, said: "[T]he public-interest considerations in accordance with the national program of fuel conservation and the difficult financial posture of transatlantic carriers, which have been aggravated by the skyrocketing increases in the cost of fuel, justify the imposition of capacity restraints as a means of maintaining capacity offered within some reasonable relationship to traffic demand".[31]

Because the carriers were unable to agree on conditions for its extension, that agreement expired at the end of the winter season.

In February 1976, the Board, in a decision particularly significant for the length of the period covered, approved a capacity reduction agreement involving service between Miami and London through April 1977. The Board took note that during the term of the agreement the two carriers on the route, British Airways and National Airlines, would operate 86 fewer round-trip flights than they would otherwise. The fuel savings over the period is estimated to

[31] U.S. Civil Aeronautics Board, Order 75-10-77, October 20, 1975, covering service through April 1976.

exceed 10 million gallons valued at about $4.5 million.[32]

As an argument for controlling excessive capacity, the need to reduce fuel consumption has instant recognition. The extremely burdensome and rising level of fuel prices since the fuel crisis began has made fuel cost an inordinately heavy element of airline operating expense, and caused a sharp rise in the load factor needed to break even, much less produce a profit. The needless waste of jet fuel is inexcusable. But so is the needless incurring of labor and other operating expenses when flight frequencies are excessive, to say nothing of the needless waste of investment capital. All of these factors, plus the unusual competitive situation in an industry in which many governments see their national interests at stake, argue for the wisdom of continuing capacity agreements in international service.

If the need for capacity limitation and the various types of cost savings it makes possible are more pressing in the North Atlantic than in most other international markets, it is because the financial distress is extreme there. Just how much of a cost savings can be realized by instituting control over the amount of scheduled

[32] U.S. Civil Aeronautics Board, Order 76-2-60, February 17, 1976, covering service through April 1977.

flight capacity operated by the carriers depends upon how much of a limitation is placed on capacity offerings. The greater the capacity cut, the greater the potential for cost reduction. Beyond some point, the public would suffer and capacity limitation would become inappropriate, but it is clear that a substantial savings can be achieved with frequency limitations having only minimal implications for flying convenience. Thus, an average reduction of but 15 per cent in the capacity offered on the North Atlantic during the past year—a cutback which would still permit abundant scheduled service—would have resulted in an increase of about 10 percentage points in the average load factor across the market—a performance improvement sufficient to have had a large effect on airline profitability.

In individual markets a cutback of greater proportions, and therefore of greater financial benefit to the airlines, is undoubtedly feasible without any real depreciation of service convenience. For example, under capacity arrangements in effect in the 1975–76 winter season, Pan American and British Airways each flew 5 non-stop flights a week in each direction between Washington and London, instead of daily flights as previously, a reduction of about 29 per cent. On the two days on which either carrier had withdrawn its flight the other maintained service at about the same time of morning (London-Washington) or evening (Washington-London). As a result, the public had available to it at normal departure times at least one flight every day via one carrier or the other and, on heavier travel days, flights offered by both carriers. Better average loads for both carriers resulted, and it can hardly be said that the public convenience was significantly affected.

In the case of Miami-London, the CAB noted that in the absence of a capacity reduction agreement "there would be severe excess capacity in the market with an average of 379 empty round-trip seats each day, and a projected seat factor (passenger load factor) of 40.8 percent". With the capacity agreement in effect, the average of empty round-trip seats is expected to drop to 84 per day, and the load factor to rise to 68.6 percent. The capacity in this market, the Board said, "is significantly in excess of that which would be adequate for traffic demands . . . Additionally, it is clear that the proposed service levels will be adequate to meet the needs of the traveling public . . . Although these load factors (68.6 percent) are high, we do not believe they are either excessive or unreasonable".[33]

The current capacity agreement between

[33] Ibid. pp. 3-6.

American and British carriers on the Miami-London route is the only capacity control now in effect on scheduled service between the United States and Europe. Capacity and revenue pooling arrangements are extant, however, between Canadian and European carriers.

While the concurrence of the CAB and of the regulatory agencies of other governments is necessary for capacity limitation agreements in the North Atlantic, regulators need to do more than merely pass upon proposed arrangements placed before them for approval. They can and should, by policy pronouncement, actively encourage capacity agreements which meet the essential tests of the public interest: significantly improving airline efficiency and reducing costs while preserving an adequate level of scheduled service.

The airlines for their part, should provide the necessary initiative for proposing and negotiating capacity arrangements in the North Atlantic on a scale more ambitious and more suited to the need for improved financial performance than the limited arrangements now in effect. Because of the overlap of potential routings, airline initiatives should preferably be pursued simultaneously as part of a broad multilateral program embracing the major submarkets of the North

Atlantic. All the carriers would stand to benefit from a general capacity cutback applied widely and more or less uniformly.

While it would be most effective, and most equitable, if all of the scheduled carriers in the market were to participate, and essentially on a ratable basis, in capacity limitation arrangements, it would be a mistake to regard achieving 100 per cent participation as a necessary condition for proceeding with such arrangements at all. The leading ten or twelve carriers account for such a large share of the total traffic in the North Atlantic, and have such a preponderant stake in the opportunities available for efficiency improvement and cost reduction through capacity limitation, that it is in their interest to agree upon broad-scale reduction of flight frequencies among themselves even if some lesser carriers in the market decline to join in the arrangement and thus try to enrich themselves from the cutbacks of the majors.

The possible loss of market share to non-participants—unjust though it may be—should not obscure the substantial gains which capacity cutbacks can achieve for those that do participate. The old warning to beware lest the best become the enemy of the good applies here. So long as the non-participants do not represent so large a share of the market as to make the entire undertaking uneconomic, a move toward achieving the substantial cost savings inherent in large-scale capacity reduction on a multilateral basis ought not to be permitted to fail for resentment over advantages that may unfairly accrue to the covetous.

Most capacity limitation arrangements in the past have been negotiated under bilateral agreements. If a broad attack is to be mounted on the problem of excess capacity in the North Atlantic market as a whole, the interrelatedness of the routes makes it highly desirable to deal with the problems on a multilateral basis. There is no formal machinery in existence for such multilateralism on capacity questions, but as with many another international matter, machinery should present no serious obstacle once the governments most concerned recognize that an urgent problem exists and determine that it must and will be met. This does not call for any change in the basic bilateral agreements by which air rights are exchanged. What is required is simply a process for coherent and collective deliberation and action to coordinate the interests of multiple governments in achieving sensible capacity limitation broadly across the North Atlantic market. A process of this kind already exists for such coordination with respect to rate matters, and it should be feasible to develop some workable mechanism to achieve capacity limitation on a broad basis when it is of such importance to do so.[34]

Another reservation sometimes expressed concerning the use of capacity limitation agreements is that the carriers may transfer the released capacity to other markets, either scheduled or charter, and thus merely shift, rather than cure, the excess capacity which the agreements are intended to remedy. This is a legitimate concern, but the problem is not peculiar to capacity agreements. The very same problem arises when frequencies on a route are reduced by parallelling unilateral actions of individual carriers and the released capacity is shifted to other routes. Nevertheless, when capacity limitation is given regulatory sanction, it is appropriate to establish safeguards to make sure that the efficiencies and economies achieved by capacity reduction in one market are not cancelled by creating inefficiencies and diseconomies in another. The standard policy of the Civil Aeronautics Board is to monitor capacity limitation

[34] The European Civil Aviation Conference may offer a means of coordinating the interests of its member governments on the subject of scheduled-capacity limitations in the North Atlantic.

arrangements by means of "reporting requirements . . . to guard against the predatory use
of freed capacity",[35] and that policy should be
continued.

A final word is in order on the relation of
capacity agreements to "pooling" arrangements.
While capacity control agreements involving
American carriers tend to be regarded in the
United States with the traditional suspicion with
which it views collective business arrangements
generally, such agreements are commonly employed by other airlines on major international
routes, including those within Europe and between Europe and other continents, where they
are frequently reinforced by some type of financial "pooling", ranging from rigid sharing of
costs and revenues to routine financial adjust-
ment for differences between agreed and actual
capacity shares operated.

Under the pooling arrangement between Air
Canada and British Airways on the Canada-
U.K. route, negotiated under the bilateral air
agreement between the two countries, each airline provides 50 per cent of an agreed total

[35] U.S. Civil Aeronautics Board, Order 76-2-60, February
17, 1976. "As the Board has repeatedly stated in the past,
the transfer of released capacity to nonagreement markets
will not be tolerated." (p. 7)

scheduled capacity on the route, their frequencies are coordinated for service coverage, revenues are shared equally, and capacity imbalances are settled by intercarrier payments at an agreed amount per seat. The total amount of capacity operated is established and regularly reviewed in light of traffic trends so as to achieve, as closely as possible, a target load factor. No restriction is placed upon other aspects of airline operation or marketing. Average load factors on the route are above those experienced in the North Atlantic generally.

Even when not supplemented by financial pooling arrangements, capacity limitation agreements can have a beneficial effect upon load factors, and can stand on their own merits independent of such arrangements. At the same time, when considering capacity limitation agreements there is no need for regulators, particularly in the United States, to shy away from considering also the ways in which financial provisions can help to make capacity limitation work more smoothly. "Pooling" has strong emotional connotations in the antitrust lexicon, and it is true that on some international routes on which pooling arrangements are in effect the airlines may well have gone too far in emphasizing load factor at the expense of service quality.

While achievement of high load factors is important, it can not forgive a serious degradation of scheduled service. The service deterioration in such cases, however, comes not from the financial arrangements which are present, but from the capacity reduction provisions they accompany.

In a basic sense, mutual capacity limitation is itself a type of pooling. The carriers, in effect, agree upon a total amount of frequency or seats to be operated and upon the allotments to the individual participants. If capacity limitation is felt by regulators to be needed in order to improve airline efficiency and reduce costs, a decision as to whether or not to include financial provisions should hinge only on whether or not these are essential to realizing the objectives of capacity limitation. If so, such provisions can be approved; if not, approval is unnecessary. In neither case is any new principle of competition at stake beyond that involved in capacity limitation itself. The inclusion of financial provisions is of secondary importance. What is of primary importance is to accomplish the urgently needed reduction of scheduled capacity in the North Atlantic as expeditiously as possible and in a manner which comports with good public service.

Integrating Scheduled and Charter Capacity

Capacity reduction to relieve the market of at least some of the flight frequencies which are excess to good public service and a needless burden on operating costs is one avenue to achieving more efficient use of air transport resources in the North Atlantic. Another and equally important approach is to use to better advantage the airline capacity that is operated by breaking down the barriers that now prevent the mixing of scheduled and charter passengers on the same flight.

Conventional distinctions between scheduled and charter service have become somewhat blurred in recent years. Scheduled service, marketed direct to the customer at retail, nominally involves the movement of individually-ticketed passengers on regularly scheduled flights. Charter service, marketed in bulk through wholesale channels (which may or may not be affiliated with the carriers), nominally involves the movement of blocks of passengers on non-scheduled flights. Charter (supplemental) airlines serve only the charter market. Scheduled airlines serve both the scheduled and the charter markets. At the low-price end of the travel spectrum, however, there is not only a substantial degree of competition between charter service and the discount-promotional categories of scheduled service, but an overlap between the quality characteristics of the two services. The charter operations of many carriers, both scheduled airlines and supplementals, are extensive enough to permit considerable regularity of charter flight departures, especially during peak travel periods. The "schedulized" nature of such charter operations reflects a type of service quality formerly associated exclusively with traditional scheduled flights. Also, with the formation of charter groups by tour organizers under liberalized eligibility rules, charter service is in many cases available on what is tantamount to, if not precisely identical with, a single-ticket basis, formerly thought of as peculiar to scheduled flights.

In catering to the low-price market, charter flights operate at or close to full load. Their full-load operation is facilitated by the right to fill up the airplane by selling "split" charters, that is, to market the seating capacity of the flight in multiple blocks, not just a single block. Scheduled service has no corresponding right and operates, on the average, far below full load.

Under present regulatory policy, scheduled and charter passengers in the North Atlantic may not be carried on the same flight. This restriction upon optimum capacity utilization is no impediment to efficient use of the capacity of charter airlines, which already operate their flights on a fully-loaded basis, but it seriously shackles efficient use of the capacity operated by scheduled airlines. Scheduled carriers, compelled to use separate aircraft for their scheduled and their charter passengers, may not fill up a scheduled flight by carrying a block of charter passengers in otherwise empty seats. As a result, it is not at all unusual for a scheduled carrier to be running a 707 charter flight at about the same time that one of its scheduled jumbo-jet flights is departing with more than enough unfilled seats to accommodate all of the passengers being carried on the charter flight.

This waste of capital, fuel, manpower, and other resources goes counter to every principle for improving productivity and imposes pointless costs upon financially weakened carriers. In the interest of maximizing efficiency and reducing costs, the scheduled airlines should be authorized to serve the full spectrum of air travel demands in the same aircraft whenever, and to the full extent that, it is economic to do so.

The capacious wide-bodied airplanes not only permit, they all but clamor for, such integration of the widest range of different types or classes of service under one cabin roof.

The economic waste inherent in the present regulatory bar against mixing scheduled and charter passengers in the same aircraft is prodigious. Over the North Atlantic system as a whole, there are several million unused scheduled seats each year. A substantial number of these seats could be filled, and operating costs dramatically lowered, if the scheduled airlines were free to utilize their flight capacity in an integrated fashion, combining scheduled and charter services on individual flights or running such services separately, solely as dictated by considerations of efficient utilization of capacity. The increased load factors which would result from permitting the scheduled airlines to make the best use of their fleets by integrating scheduled and charter services in the same aircraft— "part-chartering", as it is sometimes termed— would produce not only the operating economies associated with higher load factors but the further operating economies that would be derived from elimination of charter flights made unnecessary by the consolidation of scheduled and charter capacity.

Care would have to be taken to make certain

that the charter passengers carried on scheduled flights remained subject to the travel restrictions that now apply to charter service. The purpose of integrated utilization of scheduled and charter flight capacity would be to make more economic use of capacity, and this can be accomplished without permitting charter passengers paying charter fares to enjoy the less restrictive conditions for which scheduled passengers must pay a higher fare.

The right of a scheduled airline to carry charter passengers either on a planeload charter flight or in the otherwise empty seats of a scheduled flight would be exercised exclusively at the discretion of the airline and in the interest of employing its scheduled and charter capacity most efficiently. When it was more efficient for operating or marketing reasons to carry a particular block or blocks of charter passengers on a charter flight, the airline could do so. When it was more efficient to move such charter passengers on a scheduled flight, the airline could exercise that option. The right of the airline to utilize the more efficient alternative would not become the right of a charter passenger to travel either on a scheduled flight or a charter flight at his option. The necessary safeguards should not be difficult to arrange. Simply stated, the decision of the airline to fill up a scheduled flight with a block of charter passengers and thus make it unnecessary to operate the charter flight would not exempt the charter traveler from any of the booking, departure, return, length of stay, deposit, forfeiture or other provisions of a charter fare. Those provisions would remain the same, just as if the charter service were being provided on a planeload charter flight.

Care would also have to be taken, as in the case of capacity limitation arrangements, to make sure through regulatory restraints that the capacity released as a result of consolidation of scheduled and charter services were not destructively used in other markets.

It would be essential also to prevent the carriage of charter passengers on scheduled flights from blotting up so much scheduled seating capacity as to undermine the basic quality of scheduled service available to the traveling public that values and relies upon it. This is a problem similar to that involved in keeping agreements to limit scheduled capacity from going too far. It is a problem of balancing the interests of airline efficiency and the interests of public convenience, and entirely within the power of regulators to control. While the capacity-reduction approach and the capacity-consolidation approach improve efficiency in different ways, both would have the effect of raising load factors on scheduled flights. Harmonization between the two is needed, and any regulatory limits imposed to assure the maintenance of adequate scheduled service should be established on a coordinated basis.

The experience with integrated operation of scheduled and charter services on scheduled flights on intra-European routes, while not quite on all fours with the situation in the North Atlantic, is nevertheless instructive. Such integrated operation was begun on an experimental basis in 1971 by scheduled carriers operating between the United Kingdom and various points in Spain and Portugal, and subsequently was greatly broadened to include a wide range of destinations on the Continent. On these routes, chiefly involving holiday travel, charter traffic had become so large in relation to scheduled service as to threaten the continuation of any substantial level of such service, and "so-called 'part-charter' arrangements" were instituted as a remedial device. In affirming the continuation of such arrangements on these routes, the U.K. Civil Aviation Authority in April 1974, stating that "the essence of the 'part charter' arrangements is to give the scheduled carriers the same competitive flexibility as the charter carriers enjoy",[36] authorized the scheduled carriers to offer up to 50 per cent of the capacity of each scheduled flight (or 70 seats, if greater) on a charter basis.

A similar approach could be adopted in the North Atlantic. The space eligible for charter service on a scheduled flight could be limited to a stipulated proportion of the flight capacity or a stipulated number of seats or a combination of the two. The aim of imposing such a limitation, however, should be to safeguard the quality of the scheduled service for the traveling public and not to safeguard charter competitors.

The healthiest competition from the standpoint of the public occurs when market success is determined by the relative efficiency of rivals and when such efficiency is unimpeded by artificial restrictions. Removing barriers to efficient use of airline capacity is, without qualification, good public policy. It promotes optimum use of economic resources and lower economic costs borne by consumers. The public interest is not advanced by imposing operating inefficiencies

[36] U.K. Civil Aviation Authority, Decision on 117 Class 1B Applications by BEA, BOAC, British Caledonian, British Cambrian Airways and Northeast Airlines, listed in ATLN No. 102/2.2, April 9, 1974. Appeal dismissed by Secretary of State, December 23, 1974.

upon scheduled airlines to protect their competitors nor, for that matter, by imposing such inefficiencies upon those competitors to protect the scheduled airlines. The economics of charter operations are founded on the full or nearly full use of equipment. Even though the load factors achieved by consolidation of scheduled and charter flights would fall short of those attained in charter service, the improved use of equipment resulting from such consolidation would produce for the scheduled airlines significant cost savings no less important to the public than those the charter airlines derive from planeload charters. Cost savings based on improved efficiency always benefit one's competitive position, but in a way that also benefits the public both by conserving resources and by helping to hold down prices. Denying either to the scheduled airlines or to the public the benefits flowing from increased efficiency made possible by consolidation of scheduled and charter capacity merely to protect the charter airlines from vigorous competition would be no more justifiable than denying to the charter airlines the advantages of planeload charter operation in order to protect the scheduled carriers from the low-price competition such charter economies create.

The charter airlines have heretofore opposed

the mixing of scheduled and charter passengers on scheduled flights in the North Atlantic as "a mongrel species, born of the misalliance of the low rates made possible by full planeload economies with the unused capacity of over-scheduled services".[37] Consolidation of scheduled and charter capacity certainly involves a mating of two types of service which up to now have been operated in separate aircraft. It is a strength not a weakness of that marriage, however, that it couples the economies of planeload charter flights with the unused capacity of scheduled flights. There is, after all, nothing sacred about the continuation of the present segregation practice, nor anything unnatural about changing it. The elimination of wasteful restrictions upon operating efficiency is eternally a fit subject for regulatory interest, and the concept of consolidation of services or facilities to promote efficiency and reduce costs has many respectable and successful precedents in other industries. If adapting that concept to North Atlantic air transport can help to meet the pressing problems of the scheduled airlines in a manner that is consonant with sound economics and

[37] "Part-Charter: Panacea or Peril", Presentation by International Air Carrier Association to European Civil Aviation Conference, January 28, 1975, p. 15.

sound public policy, the parochial self-interest of the charter airlines can not be allowed to block the way. The needs of the charter airlines merit the concern of regulators just as do the needs of the scheduled airlines. There is a right way and a wrong way to meet the needs of either group, however, and the "wrongest" way is to impede one or the other from making full use of its opportunities for operating at highest efficiency and lowest cost.

The concept of mixing charter and scheduled passengers on scheduled flights has been criticized by the supplemental carriers on the ground that its adoption would adversely affect the scheduled carriers themselves through "self-diversion of traffic, declining yields, over-capacity, and eventually erosion of service to the public".[38]

The arguments concerning self-diversion and yield erosion boil down to the observation that, inasmuch as charter fares are lower than scheduled fares, passengers ordinarily using scheduled service will tend to favor the charter service when both services are available on the same flight, thus causing a loss in scheduled traffic and a decline in average yields. The answer to this argument is essentially that the mere consolida-

[38] Ibid., p. 7.

tion of scheduled and charter flights, without changing any of the conditions attaching to either scheduled or charter service, introduces no new element to influence the traveler's choice. The effect of the consolidation of the two types of service on the same flight is to produce operating economies for the airline, while leaving the travel status of the passenger unchanged.

The argument concerning deterioration of service to the public derives from the legitimate proposition that load factors on a scheduled flight could be pushed so high by the carriage of charter passengers that the qualities the public requires of a true scheduled service would be lost. As indicated earlier, the problem is controllable through effective regulation.

The argument that consolidation of scheduled and charter service would serve as a stimulus to overcapacity is based upon the premise that as the carriage of charter passengers on scheduled flights caused load factors to rise, the airlines would be tempted to add frequencies, and the ensuing expansion of capacity would, instead of curing current problems, compound them. The syndrome involved here has been discussed at length in the section of this study dealing with the need for capacity limitation agreements among the carriers. With capacity agreements, the amount of capacity operated can be sufficiently attuned to demand so as to achieve the benefits of load factors which are high enough to present substantial cost savings but not so high as to cause significant inconveniences to the public, while containing the pressures which customarily lead individual carriers to create excessive capacity in the market as a whole. The needed integration of scheduled and charter services on scheduled flights should therefore be developed in combination with capacity limitation arrangements.

The most serious concern of the charter airlines regarding consolidation of scheduled and charter flights by scheduled carriers appears to be that the charter market may be swamped with capacity as the scheduled airlines undertake to fill empty scheduled seats with charter traffic and that such swamping will grow worse if the right to mix scheduled and charter passengers in scheduled flights leads the scheduled carriers to expand their scheduled frequencies without restraint. The charter carriers are not alone in this concern. At least one scheduled carrier has expressed similar trepidation. Referring to "part-chartering" arrangements on intra-European routes, a Lufthansa official fears that "capacity planning will be based on the low-price demand" and that "available capacity will be increased to match an illusory upturn in the market."[39]

It should be stressed again that consolidation of scheduled and charter passengers on scheduled flights should proceed hand-in-glove with a program of capacity limitation. The way to prevent serious capacity excesses is by controlling the amount of capacity operated, not by preventing the airlines from employing in the most efficient manner the capacity that is operated. The purpose of integrated utilization of scheduled and charter capacity is to enable the scheduled airlines to operate more efficiently, and thus at lower cost. The purpose is not to provide them with a device for overwhelming their charter competitors with capacity thrown onto the bulk travel market or to permit them to exact a larger share of that market.

The most effective way to insulate the charter market from capacity swamping by the scheduled airlines as a concomitant of the consolidation of charter and scheduled services would be to establish quantitative limits upon the total

[39] Interview with Mr. Reinhard Bock, General Manager for Passenger Traffic and Sales, Lufthansa, Flight International Magazine, March 27, 1975, p. 520.

amount of charter capacity the scheduled airlines could operate, leaving them free to divide this amount between charter flights and scheduled flights in accordance with the best efficiency of the airlines. These limits would be established annually and would be matched by a corresponding limitation upon the amount of charter capacity operated by the charter airlines. This subject is explored in greater detail in the section immediately following.

Controlling Charter Capacity

The charter airlines strongly favor any measure for controlling the amount of scheduled capacity operated. They strongly oppose any measure for controlling charter capacity. A rational and effective regulatory system for achieving efficient use of airline capacity in the North Atlantic requires control of both. In the competitive realities of the struggle for business, the total capacity in the market plays a crucial role. A regulatory scheme for controlling capacity can not be effective unless it encompasses the capacity offered by both rivaling forces, not just one.

The main competition between scheduled and charter airlines, and between scheduled and charter services, occurs in the low-price categories of the travel market. The charter carriers compete in the low-price market with their charter services, while the scheduled carriers compete in that market both with their charter services and with the discount-promotional categories of their scheduled services. The low-price end of the market now accounts for the lion's share of air travel across the North Atlantic. Only about one-fifth of total North Atlantic passenger traffic travels at first-class or normal economy fares. The remaining four-fifths of the traffic consists of budget-conscious passengers traveling either on charter flights or at some type of discount or promotional fare on scheduled flights.[40] Charter service accounts for about one-third of the total low-price market, and charter airlines supply about 60 per cent of total charter service.[41]

Controlling the amount of scheduled capacity overhanging the low-price air travel market would benefit charter as well as scheduled airlines. But control of scheduled capacity without some control over charter capacity is not work-

[40] Detail in Appendix Table 2.
[41] Detail in Appendix Tables 2 and 3.

able. If charter airlines remained free to expand their capacity while scheduled competitors contracted theirs, the imbalance would undermine the effectiveness of scheduled-capacity control, to the detriment of both segments of the industry.

The fifteen- to twenty-fold increase in the traffic carried by the charter airlines over the past decade is both a measure and a result of the emergence of new competitive forces in the North Atlantic. The competitive battle between scheduled and charter airlines in the low-price travel market has been carried on by means of capacity and price and the interaction of the two. Proliferation of capacity offerings of the charter airlines and of the charter and discount-promotional offerings of the scheduled carriers has brought prices under strong competitive pressure, and the traffic generated by low prices has induced a heavy buildup of capacity by both competing groups.

With respect to the operation of scheduled capacity controls, the charter airlines take the position that regulatory restrictions are needed to make sure that capacity freed from scheduled service is not thrown into the North Atlantic charter market. As a matter of policy, and partially in response to the representations of the charter airlines, capacity limitation agreements approved by the Civil Aeronautics Board are monitored to make sure that such transfers do not occur. As suggested earlier, similar conditions would be appropriate in the broader undertaking that is needed for limiting scheduled capacity in the North Atlantic market as a whole. It would make neither regulatory nor economic sense, however, to shrink scheduled capacity, and to bar the scheduled airlines from shifting into their charter operations any of the capacity so eliminated, if the charter airlines could expand their own capacity offerings at will, particularly when, as indicated earlier, many charter airlines have already achieved sufficient regularity to allow a fair degree of flight scheduling of their own. Such an anomaly might serve the competitive interests of the charter-specializing airlines, but it cannot meet the test of balanced, consistent regulatory policy. And if, as is likely, the contradiction in the end caused a collapse of scheduled capacity arrangements, or precluded their successful negotiation in the first place, all of the carriers—scheduled and supplemental alike—would be the losers.

Earlier it was observed that limitation of scheduled frequencies under capacity agreements could be beneficial to the participating

scheduled carriers even if some scheduled carriers at the periphery of the market declined to
join in the limitation and thus earned unjust
advantages at the expense of the participants.
The situation is different as between scheduled
and charter carriers. The competitive importance of the charter airlines is of central, not
peripheral, importance in the market. The charter airlines often point out that despite their
impressive growth, their total passenger volume
is still a "minor" factor in total North Atlantic
traffic. From a competitive standpoint, of course,
the relevant market is the low-price segment of
North Atlantic traffic, and the head-to-head
competition of the charter carriers with both
the charter and discount-promotional services of
the scheduled airlines dynamically affects the
entire structure of services and fares across that
market. The one-third of the low-price air
travel market which the charter airlines represent is, technically, still the minor share of the
market, but that minority is of such consequence
for basic competitive relationships that it cannot be ignored in any program for controlling
capacity.

Controls on charter capacity should operate
alongside controls on scheduled capacity and
should apply equally to the charter services of

the scheduled and of the supplemental airlines. The purpose of such controls should be to prevent capacity excesses in the charter market and to insure a properly coordinated effort to achieve the most efficient utilization of air transport resources in the North Atlantic. Their purpose should not be to ration travelers who wish to use charter service, nor to force travel onto scheduled service for lack of availability of charters.

An effective system of charter-capacity controls would involve the establishment of quantitative ceilings on total charter capacity for all major city-pair markets in the North Atlantic— the same markets to which controls on scheduled capacity would apply. These city-pairs would be grouped, regionally, or otherwise, wherever necessary to conform to geographic market realities, and for this purpose such groupings could be extremely broad. The quotas would be determined by regulatory decision on the basis of the amount of capacity judged to be required to fulfill public demands for charter services. The quotas established for each market grouping would be varied directionally and seasonally, and allocated to individual carriers, both scheduled and non-scheduled, by means of quantitative licenses to operate charter capacity in the market or markets concerned. Capacity allotments to the carriers would be based in the first instance upon carrier applications for such licenses, and where a quota was oversubscribed the distribution of licenses among individual carriers would be based upon their historical participation in the traffic. To maintain opportunities for new entrants, a suitable portion of each quota would be reserved for licensing to carriers with no previous participation in the market.

Similar control approaches have in the past been used to good effect by governments in analogous circumstances. A conspicuous example is the successful program used to administer export controls in the United States during the period after World War II. Although the objective was somewhat different, the system employed to establish quantitative quotas in geographic markets and to allocate by license to individual claimants can be readily adapted in devising a workable program of charter-capacity controls in the North Atlantic.[42]

As in the case of controls over scheduled ca-

---

[42] "Export Control and Allocation Powers", Sixth Quarterly Report by the Secretary of Commerce to the President, the Senate, and House of Representatives, January 31, 1949, and prior Quarterly Reports.

pacity, applying charter-capacity controls across a broad market such as the North Atlantic involves the interests of several governments and will require a multilateral process of discussion and negotiation. The European Civil Aviation Conference has been active in matters involving the charter policies of its member governments, and may well provide appropriate intergovernmental machinery for coordinating the interests of the various European governments with those of the United States and Canada.

The non-scheduled airlines have argued strongly against permitting the integration of scheduled and charter services on scheduled flights on the ground that it could lead to the scheduled airlines' swamping the charter market with a great new source of charter capacity. A program of charter-capacity controls along the lines envisaged here would eliminate these fears. It would fix the amount of charter capacity which the scheduled airlines could operate, just as it would fix the amount of capacity the charter airlines could operate. The charter-capacity quota set for the scheduled airlines would be designed to limit them to the amount of such capacity they would ordinarily operate whether or not they had the right to consolidate scheduled and charter services. The scheduled airlines would merely have the option to operate their charter-capacity quota either in planeload charter flights as at present or in the unused seats of scheduled flights. Thus, the scheduled airlines would be enabled to use their combined scheduled and charter capacity so as to maximize their operating efficiency, while the non-scheduled airlines would be protected from the menace of capacity swamping, and the interests of the entire industry would be advanced.

III

Achieving Economic Fares

COROLLARY to more efficient use of capacity as a remedy for the ills of air transport in the North Atlantic is achieving a system of fares which both reflects and supports economic efficiency. Conditions for holding down prices the public must pay for air transport are most favorable when the operating and capital costs that must be covered by airline revenues are minimized by efficient use of resources. And, of course, economically efficient air transport can be sustained only if revenues are adequate to cover the operating and capital costs of supplying an efficient service.

Assuming that the measures proposed for achieving improved efficiency in the North Atlantic through better employment of flight capacity are successfully put into effect, what principles should govern the establishment and regulation of airline fares? The answer to that question can best be approached in terms of the three basic aspects of the mater: fares for scheduled services, fares for charter services, and the relationship of scheduled and charter fares to each other.

Fares for Scheduled Services

As in the case of air fares in international scheduled service generally, scheduled fares between Europe and North America are established through a process of industry accord, subject to the approval of affected governments. The process, whatever its imperfections, meets a political and practical necessity.

Almost universally, governments tend to use their control of landing rights to protect or advance national interests in international air traffic touching their shores. Under bilateral air agreements for exchange of these rights, fares for airline service between two countries must have the blessing of both governments. There are,

however, formidable practical difficulties in setting fares bilaterally where, as in the case of
the North Atlantic, the market is comprised of
many different—and directly or indirectly competitive—pairings of countries, and where routings frequently involve service to intermediate
or prior or subsequent points in one or more
other countries. Some mechanism for multilateral determination of related fares is imperative.
Partly because of the financial and marketing
complexities surrounding the rate-making process, and partly to minimize the occasion for gov-
ernment-to-government confrontations on air
fares, the procedure has been to rely upon the
airlines to negotiate fare agreements among
themselves initially, with the governments re-
taining both the opportunity to influence these
negotiations and the authority to approve or dis-
approve the final results. The International Air
Transport Association provides the industry
conference machinery for this multilateral negotiation of rates for scheduled services, and the
multiple bilateral government approvals given
to country-to-country rates provides the needed
intergovernmental endorsement.[1]

[1] "The International Air Transport Association, a re-
constituted version of the prewar International Air Traffic
Association, was recognized as a suitable organization to

Any mechanism intended to fulfill the un-
orthodox role of multilateral price negotiation
under the conditions which characterize scheduled air service among nations is bound to produce results which are less than ideal. Alleged
pricing failures or inadequacies blamed on
IATA are more often than not attributable to
the intrinsic difficulties of collective rate-making
in a service industry comprised of firms of dis-
parate nationality, size, and route structure, all
subject to regulation by, and many directly
owned by, their governments. In these circumstances, it has been remarked, difficult pricing
problems would arise "even if the procedures of
IATA were perfect and the Conferences were
presided over by the Archangel Gabriel".[2]

provide the machinery for reaching inter-airline agreements on fares . . . The emerged structure is one based
on bilateral agreements between countries, negotiated by
national airlines and sanctioned by the respective governments. The authority to fix international fares is derived
from these intergovernment agreements, and it is the fare
clause in these agreements which established IATA-fixed
fares. Thus, the IATA-fixed fares spread multilaterally by
means of bilateral agreements." A. P. Ellison and E. M.
Stafford, "The Dynamics of the Civil Aviation Industry",
Saxon House (D. C. Heath Ltd.), Westmead (Hants),
1974, pp. 7–8.

[2] Stephen Wheatcroft, "The Growing Conflict between
Scheduled Service and Charter Pricing Policies", paper
presented at the International Symposium on Transporta-

It is significant, however, that no one has yet come forward with a workable and politically acceptable alternative which differs in basic terms from the present system.[3] Even stern critics of IATA are impelled to recognize that in international scheduled air service the only, and comfortless, alternative to a system of industry conference rate-making with government review is a system of direct intergovernmental bargaining. As one such critic acknowledges, "[N]othing appears to be gained by substituting government bargaining . . . in place of the present conference procedure. The airlines themselves are best suited to this task".[4]

Unlike fares for scheduled services, charter fares are not established by industry-wide agreement but by independent pricing actions of the

---

tion, Washington, D.C., June 1969. Reprinted in M. L. Fair and J. R. Nelson, "Criteria for Transport Pricing", Cornell Maritime Press, Cambridge, Md., 1973, p. 312.

[3] The political and practical weaknesses of proposals which are occasionally put forth for totally eliminating IATA and replacing it with unrestricted price competition are best revealed by examination of the proposals themselves. See, for example, M. H. Cooper and A. K. Maynard, "The Price of Air Travel", Hobart Paper 53, The Institute for Economic Affairs, London, 1971.

[4] Mahlon R. Straszheim, "The International Airline Industry", Brookings Institution, Washington, D.C., 1969, p. 197.

individual scheduled or supplemental airlines offering charter service. As in the case of scheduled fares, however, charter fares are subject to government review.

With airlines responsible for initiating prices and regulators for reviewing them, it is important for both groups to be guided by common principles of pricing soundness. Conceptually, at least, there should be no difference between what is sound airline economics and what is sound public policy. Stated in broadest terms, the two are harmonized when fares as a whole return the full economic cost of efficient operation, but no more than such cost, and fares for individual categories of service are responsive to elasticities of demand and competitive with rival transport, but no lower than incremental or marginal costs.

That rates as a whole must fully cover costs as a whole, including a reasonable profit, is so basic as to seem elementary. Airline marketers and regulators, however, do not always appreciate that for pricing to be sound the costs that must be covered relate to the "economic", not the "accounting", costs of the enterprise.

Douglas and Miller, describing principles of efficient pricing of air transport service, call attention to the "classic distinction between economic and accounting costs" and emphasize that "for efficiency to obtain, prices must reflect economic costs".[5] The economic cost of resources consumed in providing air service "must be measured by their opportunity cost".[6] "Opportunity cost" is the economist's shorthand for the fundamental principle that the real cost of any resource used in production at any given time is represented by the value of the resource in an alternative employment, and that value is reflected in the prevailing price of the resource at the time of its use.

Costs can be divided into two main categories —operating costs and capital costs. For airlines, the difference between economic and accounting measures of cost hinges mostly on the treatment of two elements: depreciation cost, which reflects the consumption of physical capital and can be viewed as either a capital cost or an operating cost,[7] and the costs of debt and equity

[5] George W. Douglas and James C. Miller, III, "Economic Regulation of Domestic Air Transport", Brookings Institution, Washington, D.C., 1974, p. 64.

[6] Ibid., p. 63.

[7] Although depreciation is usually regarded as an operating cost, Bonbright, among others, regards depreciation as properly a capital cost. James C. Bonbright, "Principles of Public Utility Rates", Columbia University Press, 1952, p. 320.

capital. For other elements of costs—wages, fuel or miscellaneous materials and services—there is ordinarily little, if any, difference between accounting and economic measures of cost.

Turning first to depreciation, it is evident that in a period of steep and sustained inflation fare levels designed to recover capital-consumption costs calculated on asset values reflecting past rather than present price for acquiring flight equipment and constructing ground facilities are increasingly out of touch with economic reality. From the standpoint of economic efficiency, prices must generate revenues adequate to cover production costs which include an allowance for depreciation based on the cost of re-creating the equivalent productive capability of the assets at today's market prices. To reflect economic cost, the basis on which the depreciation charge is calculated must be the current replacement cost of the fixed assets, not their historic or original acquisition cost. Ryan touches the essence of the matter when he says that "a going firm . . . must calculate its costs for the ensuing period on the same basis as it would use if it were now replacing all the resources at its disposal".[8]

With respect to the costs of debt and equity

[8] W. J. L. Ryan, "Price Theory", Macmillan, London, 1964, pp. 309–310.

capital which must be covered by prices, the principle which applies corresponds to that for other resources. In economic terms, today's true cost of the long-term capital investment in an enterprise is not the "embedded" historic cost of that capital but today's market cost of obtaining the investment capital required to re-create the productive capability of the enterprise. For example, the proper cost of debt capital that a firm must cover with today's revenues is measured by "the rate or interest that it would now have to pay to induce people to buy its bonds".[9] As Joskow of M.I.T. emphasizes in dealing with the question in the case of electricity pricing, the capital costs to be included in determining prices are "*current* interest and equity costs".[10] (Emphasis in original) The principle, as mentioned earlier, is that the cost of any resource used is measured by its opportunity cost. The opportunity cost of an enterprise for debt capital is measured by its current interest rate for long-term money. Conceptually, the opportu-

[9] Ryan, ibid., p. 310.
[10] Paul L. Joskow, "Applying Economic Principles to Public Utility Rate Structures: The Case of Electricity", in C. J. Cicchetti and J. L. Jurewitz, eds., "Studies in Electric Utility Regulation", Ballinger, Cambridge, Mass., 1975, p. 47.

nity cost of equity capital—the profit or return on ownership investment—is the competitive or "normal" return on equity, and that return increases with the proportion of debt to equity in the total capital structure.

(In the United States, the United Kingdom, and elsewhere, generally-accepted accounting principles are now rapidly evolving toward a substantial degree of conformity with economic concepts.[11] The Securities and Exchange Commission recently adopted a rule requiring that corporate reports filed with it for 1976 and later years be based on current as well as historic costs, and the Financial Accounting Standards Board, the principles-setting body of the accounting profession, is in the last stages of an official review of proposals to reflect current price levels in certified financial statements. Similar movements are far advanced in the United Kingdom and other countries. Official approbation of current-value financial reporting should lead to broader recognition of economic costs by managements and regulatory

[11] For a more extensive discussion of accounting and economic concepts of cost, profit, and investment, including references to the extensive literature on the subject, see Jesse J. and Murray N. Friedman, "Relative Profitability and Monopoly Power", in Conference Board Record, December 1972, pp. 49–58.

authorities for the purpose of determining airline prices and profitability.[12])

While successful business operation and effective public policy are at one in requiring that the revenues generated by fares as a whole cover the economic costs of the service as a whole, neither the interest of the enterprise nor the interest of the public requires that each individual category of service must be priced on the basis of its fully-allocated proportion of total economic costs. Nor is it necessary, regardless of the cost standard applied, that fare-cost relationships be the same for each category. In fact, given the cost and demand characteristics of the different types or classes of air transport service in the North Atlantic, pricing each service in strict accordance with fully-allocated costs or

---

[12] In the United Kingdom, where the Civil Aviation Act 1971 establishes "an economic return to investors on the sums invested" as a standard of airline regulation, regulatory authorities apparently interpret this to mean a return based upon replacement-cost rather than original-cost asset values. In the United States, the CAB still relies upon original-cost values in computing profit and investment. Under a recent enactment of Congress, the Railroad Revitalization and Regulatory Reform Act of 1976, the Interstate Commerce Commission is to establish the revenue of railroads (and, by implication, other surface modes) needed to "provide a flow of net income plus depreciation adequate to support prudent capital outlays . . . and cover the effects of inflation".

to return uniform profit margins is ordinarily both poor business practice and out of line with efficient allocation of economic resources.

The point is particularly applicable to the scheduled carriers, which offer a wide spectrum of service-quality gradations, ranging from the privileges that go with a first-class ticket to planeload travel under charter rules. The economy cabin of a North Atlantic flight typically carries some passengers traveling on a normal-fare basis and many more on a variety of discount-promotional fare arrangements involving length-of-stay, advance-purchase, group-inclusive-tour, or other restrictions. It makes no difference whether the issue relates to a scheduled airline's pricing of its scheduled in comparison with its charter services, or of its first class vis-a-vis its economy scheduled services, or of one type of economy service in relation to others. So long as the fare for each category recovers at least its incremental or marginal cost and thus contributes to profit—and so long as fares as a whole do not produce an excessive profit—price differentiation which sustains or stimulates traffic and revenues by catering to different public wants and needs or by meeting competition serves the business good and the public good.

In support of fully-allocated costs as the

standard of pricing of individual segments of output, it is sometimes argued that such a standard, by assigning to each segment some part of all costs, will insure that total costs, including a reasonable profit, will be covered. The argument does not stand close examination. The elasticity of demand in response to price can not be ignored. Establishing a price to equate with a fully-allocated cost omits two dynamic and crucial factors from the equation: the effect of price upon demand and the effect of demand, i.e., volume, upon unit costs and thus upon price. A large proportion of airline costs are unallocable among individual service categories except in the most arbitrary manner. But even if this were not so, pricing each category on an inflexible fully-allocated-cost basis would produce the perverse result that consumers at higher levels of the price-quality spectrum would be charged less for air travel than they were able and willing to pay, while consumers at lower levels of that spectrum would be prevented by price from traveling even though the airline would be more profitable—or less unprofitable—by carrying them at lower fares than not carrying them at all. As Baumol points out, "[F]ully distributed cost pricing can be inimical to the interest of the firm, the consuming public, and the general welfare . . . [T]he fact is that no cost calculation can guarantee the profitability of a service; that depends also on the state of demand".[13]

Price, Joseph Schumpeter once said, is "a coefficient of economic choice", meaning that consumers, by the prices they are willing to pay, show their preferences among the range of goods or services they are offered and "at the point at which they stop buying, the price will exactly measure that preference for every one of them".[14] In the private and the public interest alike, sensitivity to consumer preferences is crucial to sound product pricing, and in no industry is this more true than in one dedicated to serving the public.

Some travelers on scheduled flights are willing to pay for the advantages associated with first-class or normal-economy passage; others are willing to accept various degrees of inconvenience in travel arrangements—returning in a stipulated period, booking well in advance, trav-

[13] W. J. Baumol, "Rate Making: Incremental Costing and Equity Considerations", in H. M. Trebing, ed., "Essays on Public Utility Pricing and Regulation", Michigan State University Press, Lansing, Mich., 1971, pp. 144–145.

[14] Joseph A. Schumpeter, "The Nature and Necessity of a Price System", as reprinted in D. R. Kamerschen, ed., "Readings in Microeconomics", Wiley, New York, 1969, p. 5.

eling in a group—for the advantages of a lower price; still others accept the still tighter restrictions of charter travel in return for a still lower price. Some would not travel at all if a low-price low-quality alternative that accords with their preference were not available; others would opt to use such an alternative even though, in its absence, they would be prepared to travel under a higher-quality higher-price plan. Identifying, mapping, and responding to varying degrees of consumer preference for different price-quality combinations are part of the airlines' obligation to serve the public well. In a system of pricing which is efficiently attuned to these differences in elasticity of demand, prices must be set much closer to cost where demand is highly reactive to price than where it is not, and the result is to produce varying margins of profit in different categories of service.

The economic principle involved arises from the importance of striving for the best allocation of resources within the limitations imposed by necessarily imperfect economic conditions. This is a matter of achieving "second-best" or "quasi-optimal" economic results where the optimum of the ideal world is unattainable. The economic criteria of efficient pricing under the second-best circumstances of real economic life are applicable to many industries. Where the objective is for prices as a whole to cover total costs, including a reasonable but not excessive profit, and marginal costs of individual services can not cover total costs, the rule is clear that the prices charged for those services should deviate from their costs inversely to the relative flexibility of consumer demand for them:

"Suppose a firm is required to meet some pre-stated profit requirement, e.g., it is required to cover all of its costs including its cost of capital. If this result is not attained by prices equal to marginal costs, then consumers' surplus from the consumption of the outputs in question will be maximized if ... prices are set ... equal to the inverse ratio of the elasticities of demand."[15]

"[T]he social welfare will be served most effectively [when] items with elastic demands are priced at levels close to their marginal costs. The prices of items whose demands are inelastic diverge from their marginal costs by relatively wider margins."[16]

[15] William J. Baumol, "Reasonable Rules for Rate Regulation: Plausible Policies for an Imperfect World", in Almarin Phillips and Oliver E. Williamson, eds., "Prices: Issues in Theory, Practice, and Public Policy", University of Pennsylvania Press, Philadelphia, 1967, p. 122.

[16] William J. Baumol and David F. Bradford, "Optimal Departures from Marginal Cost Pricing", in American Economic Review, June 1970, p. 267. For further amplifi-

Economic efficiency thus calls for lower profit margins on those classes of service in which price makes a big difference in the level of demand, and higher profit margins where demand is less affected by price. This rule of efficient pricing applies particularly in the case of North Atlantic air transport, where a significant portion of total costs is not realistically allocable to the various services and the added cost of carrying added traffic which can fill otherwise empty seats in expensive aircraft is low.

Determining the relative elasticities of consumer demand for various price-quality combinations is, of course, not a matter of science but of judgment, fed by experience. It is too much to expect that the rule of efficient pricing can be applied with pinpoint precision. As Turvey says in a related context, "if the rules are to be of any practical use they must not require . . . enterprises to know things which it is in practice impossible for them to ascertain".[17] What is called for is not an infallible

cation of this principle, see the list of references appended to this article and to Joskow, op. cit.; also see J. R. Nelson, ed., "Marginal Cost Pricing in Practice", Prentice-Hall, Englewood Cliffs, N.J., 1964.

[17] Ralph Turvey, "Economic Analysis and Public Enterprises", Allen and Unwin, London, 1971, p. 21.

reading of consumer preferences or a mathematical accommodation of prices to demand elasticities but a pricing policy which operates broadly in line with the spirit of efficient pricing, so that, even though the percentage deviation from marginal cost in each segment is not, with exactitude, inversely proportional to its elasticity of demand, price is, in general, set more above marginal cost in segments of the market considered less elastic than in those considered more elastic.

The present pricing policy of the scheduled airlines in the North Atlantic looks generally in this direction, with various fare plans of a lower-price lower-quality type designed to appeal to travelers with modest means and to meet charter competition. The fares in these discount-promotional categories are scaled downward from normal economy fares, depending upon the travel restrictions which apply. The Civil Aeronautics Board, however, has for some time expressed misgivings about such pricing. In a recent Statement on Passenger Fare Matters, for example, the Board voiced "serious reservations as to the practice of charging normal-fare passengers fares which are substantially in excess of fully allocated costs, in order to subsidize the carriage of other passengers at fares below cost";

characterized promotional fares as "loss-leader pricing tactics"; and urged that "the spread between normal economy fares and promotional fares be narrowed".[18]

Behind this declaration lie three misconceptions:

First is the erroneous notion that fares must not depart from fully-allocated costs. The faultiness of that view has already been discussed.

Second, and related to the first, is the mistaken idea that a fare below fully-allocated costs loses money, and that such a fare is particularly reprehensible when another fare is above fully-allocated costs.

The terms "below cost" and "loss leader" represent a confusion in thinking. So long as promotional fares are above incremental cost, they produce a profit, not a loss, in the vital sense that profits would be lower, or losses higher, if the traffic is carried than if it is not. The profit may be lower than that yielded by other fares but, as the discussion heretofore has demonstrated, differences in margin are quite consistent with economic soundness.

The fares may be lower than a hypothetical

[18] Statement of the Civil Aeronautics Board on Passenger Fare Matters to be negotiated at the IATA Worldwide Traffic Conference in Nice/Cannes, October 1975.

fully-allocated cost (hypothetical because of the unallocability of a substantial portion of cost), but the sin is a meaningless one because there is nothing sacred about fully-allocated cost pricing. If departures from the standard are not unsound, then there are only three possibilities: 1) all fares must be below fully-allocated costs, in which case an enterprise would be sentenced to operate at an inadequate profit if not an outright loss; or 2) all fares must be above fully-allocated costs (which by definition include a normal return on capital), in which case an enterprise would be encouraged to operate at an excessive profit; or 3) some fares must be above, and some below, fully-allocated costs, in which case there must obviously be a "spread" among them.

As developed earlier, pricing a line of products or services to yield varying profit margins is a commonplace in industry. The profit margin on an economy-model refrigerator, for example, is lower than that on a luxury model, and the "spread" is quite consistent with principles of efficient pricing and consumer welfare. Similarly, the price for superior cuts of meat is higher than for inferior cuts from the very same carcass, and these prices reflect demand relationships, not cost relationships.

Third is the fallacy that pricing in varying ratio to costs means that passengers in the market segment carrying the higher profit margin are "subsidizing" passengers in the segment with the lower margin, indeed that the higher margin is built into the first segment "in order" to subsidize the second. This is "subsidization" only in the most technical and limited sense. The terminology fails to convey the important truth that, but for the cost absorption and profit contribution by the "subsidized" passengers, the unit costs borne by—and thus the fares paid by —the "subsidizing" passengers would be higher. The situation is fundamentally different from the case where a route, such as the North Atlantic, on which losses are being sustained, is of central importance in the route structure of an airline and is being "carried" despite these losses by dint of profits earned on other routes.

The supplemental airlines have also registered objections to the difference in price-to-cost relationships as between normal-economy and discount-promotional services:

"In recent years, the scheduled airlines have introduced a wide array of such discount fares . . . which are prices substantially below the levels of so-called 'normal' fares . . . Passengers utilizing these discount fares receive essentially the same service as normal-fare passengers. They ride on the same airplanes, sit in the same cabins, receive the same meals and other amenities. They do not, however, pay their full share of the cost of the service they are getting . . . Each class or type of service should bear its own costs, and each passenger should pay for the service he gets."[19]

The gist of this argument has been dealt with in discussing the line of thinking contained in the CAB statement. Two additional points, however, merit special comment.

First, it is not correct that passengers traveling on discount fares "receive essentially the same service" as those paying higher fares. The rationale of the range of price-quality combinations offered by scheduled airlines is to appeal to different segments of the market so that the preferences of consumers willing to receive less in return for paying less are accommodated. In each case, a lower fare is associated with a lower quality of service; the lower the fare, the more restrictive the conditions of travel.

Second, while pricing which yields different profit margins for different categories of service

[19] Statement of National Air Carrier Association, February 25, 1975, Hearings on Oversight of Civil Aeronautics Board, U.S. Senate Subcommittee on Administrative Practices and Procedures, Washington, D.C. 94th Congress, 1st Session, pp. 1283–1285.

entails a form of economic "discrimination" among classes of consumers patronizing one service as against another, there is no discrimination among individual consumers within each class. Every passenger pays the same fare as every other passenger traveling under the same conditions.

Relation of Scheduled to Charter Fares

At the core of the controversy between scheduled and supplemental airlines about the level of discount-promotional fares is the impact of such fares upon the ongoing competitive struggle between them in the low-price sector of the North Atlantic air travel market. That sector, comprising charter as well as discount-promotional traffic, has expanded dynamically. Whereas in 1963, North Atlantic air travel was about equally divided between the budget-conscious categories of charter and discount-promotional service and the higher-fare categories of first-class and normal-economy service, the low-price sector accounted for about 90 per cent of the traffic growth over the next twelve years and in 1975 accounted for about four-fifths of the total number of passengers flying the North Atlantic. Charter service accounts for one-fourth of the total traffic, with supplementals carrying 60 per cent, and scheduled airlines 40 per cent, of the charter business. Scheduled flights carry three-fourths of the total traffic; and three-fourths of the scheduled traffic moves on discount-promotional fares.[20]

With the more price-sensitive categories of travel so dominant a factor in the total North Atlantic market, the competitive implications of pricing practices are particularly acute for both groups of competitors. The challenge to regulatory policy is to preserve for the benefit of the public a state of strenuous but healthy competition between scheduled and charter airlines.

The pricing of discount-promotional scheduled services is of major importance in the competition between scheduled and supplemental carriers. The ability of the scheduled airlines to differentiate in price-cost relationships for various services can serve either to invigorate or to undermine the competition with their smaller and more specialized rivals. It is important, for example, that the public receive the tangible benefits accruing from energetic efforts by the scheduled airlines to fight for the favor of price-

[20] Detail in Appendix Tables 2 and 3.

conscious travelers. It is equally important to safeguard the supplemental airlines from scheduled pricing policies which may be predatory or unfair. If scheduled carriers are prevented from actively competing for price-sensitive traffic by trimming their profit margins in those segments of the market, the public loses out. But if that profit-trimming takes a form which prevents the supplementals from asserting the advantages associated with the specialized nature of their operations, the public loses also. There is neither justification for permitting the scheduled carriers to overwhelm the supplementals by sheer power tactics, nor justification for maintaining for the supplemental carriers a bastion of privileged traffic walled off from the forceful competition of scheduled airlines.

Balancing these considerations is not an easy task for regulators. The course dictated by economic soundness is to encourage vigorous price competition whenever that competition derives from economic efficiency. Maintaining or expanding traffic and revenues by offering consumers varying price-quality service combinations that provide a competitive alternative to charter service is simply one aspect of airline responsiveness to different demand elasticities in different segments of the market. Discount-promotional scheduled traffic and charter traffic are both sensitive to price, and the fare charged for one or the other affects both the willingness of consumers to make a trip and the choice as between a scheduled or a charter flight. As the earlier discussion makes clear, provided that the stricture against pricing any service below its incremental cost is observed, pricing discount-promotional traffic below fully-allocated costs and maintaining lower fare-to-cost relationships for such traffic than for regular-fare categories of travel when such pricing is in line with elasticity of consumer demand is not only consistent with, but demanded by, principles of efficiency. Such price-responsiveness serves the well-being of consumers and promotes the best attainable allocation of economic resources. No one has suggested that present discount-promotional fares fail to cover incremental costs, and from a cost standpoint there appears to be no sound economic reason for interfering with such fares unless that floor is breached.

A strong argument, however, can be made that competitive relationships between scheduled and supplemental airlines need to be taken into account, in addition to cost, in determining an appropriate floor for discount-promotional fares. The relevance of this additional factor arises from the competitive leverage which a broad traffic base, coupled with the power to discriminate in profit margins among classes of consumers, confers upon the scheduled carriers in relation to the narrowly-based supplementals.

In the absence of scheduled-supplemental competition, only the scheduled carrier's cost, the price-sensitivity of various segments of the market, and the overall profit constraint would be of significance in determining the fares to be charged in those segments. But the susceptibility of a small specialized competitor to the power of a larger firm with a broad product line to lower its prices selectively on those components of the larger firm's line that compete directly with the narrowly-based rival poses something of a dilemma for sound regulatory policy. Vigorous competition requires that the scheduled carrier should be free to charge fares for discount-promotional travel which are competitive with charter travel if such fares are above incremental cost. But suppose that the incremental cost of discount-promotional service is lower than the fares charged by supplemental operators. If no restriction is placed upon incremental-cost pricing of low-fare scheduled services in such a case, charter fares will be driven down to the level of the scheduled carrier's incremental cost, at which level it may be impossible for the supplementals to survive.

The correct regulatory solution for such a dilemma in the interest of assuring both healthy competition and low prices to which the public is entitled, is a policy which permits the scheduled airlines to establish discount-promotional fares "as low as necessary" to meet charter competition, subject to two conditions: that such fares a) are above incremental costs and b) are "no lower than necessary" to meet the competition. Such a rule steers a prudent course between the dangers which unrestrained discount-promotional pricing would pose for the economic security of the supplementals and the development of charter service in general and the dangers which would be posed for the economic soundness and development of scheduled operations and the choices available to consumers if the scheduled airlines were handcuffed in their efforts to compete on a price basis in the low-price sectors now comprising so much of the total North Atlantic market.

The principle here relates not so much to the question of economic efficiency *per se* as to the desirability of maintaining a healthy competitive equilibrium between scheduled and charter services (although in a larger sense, of course, healthy competition and economic efficiency are closely related to each other). Such a principle of competitive equilibrium is consistent with well-established competition policy in other economic activities. In the unregulated sector in the United States, for example, a seller's price discrimination which adversely affects its rivals is nevertheless lawful either if the lower price is cost-justified or if the lower price is established in good faith to meet the equally low price of such rivals. A discriminatory price which undercuts the price of a rival, however, is judged unlawful. A similar principle obtains in the regulated field. In the case of surface transportation, for example, there is a basic presumption—going back to the original passage of the Interstate Commerce Act in 1887—against a railroad's charging less for a longer haul than for a shorter haul of the same commodity on the same route, except that even such a classic form of discrimination is excused from the prohibition when the lower rate on the longer route is necessary, but no lower than necessary, to meet the competition of barge lines on a water route connecting the same originating and terminating points.[21]

[21] "Section 4 of the Act . . . delimits our authority to grant relief from the long-and-short haul provision . . .

A special problem could arise in applying the standard of "no lower than necessary to meet the competition" if a discount-promotional fare, above incremental cost, is set at a level equal to the going charter fare. The question which may then come into play is whether such a discount-promotional fare level is, in terms of market reality, below the point necessary to meet the charter competition when allowance is made for the comparative consumer appeal of traveling under less restrictive conditions on a scheduled flight as against the more restrictive conditions applicable to a charter flight. A persuasive argument can be made that the point of competitive equilibrium is the point at which, with price and quality-of-service factors considered, the competing services are deemed to be equally attractive to the travelling public in terms of the consumer satisfactions and costs associated with them, and that the rate for discount-promotional scheduled service should be kept from going below this point—the point at which, taking into

Competition has been the principal special case we have recognized in granting relief . . . We have construed the . . . restrictive provision as implying, among other things, that a rate must be no lower than necessary to meet existing competition." (Anthracite Coal to New England Territory, 277 I.C.C. 569) The basic decision is Transcontinental Cases of 1922, 74 I.C.C. 48.

account the difference between scheduled and charter service in consumer appeal, the airlines supplying the rival forms of service enjoy equality of competitive opportunity for the traffic. This is the way in which the meeting-competition concept is applied in the U.S. unregulated economy in discrimination situations involving competition between premium and standard products. The same approach is used in determining the floor for railroad rates in cases involving long-and-short-haul discrimination; rail transportation is regarded as offering a quality-of-service advantage over barge transport, and the discrimination is tolerated only if an equilibrating differential, sometimes roughly determined, is maintained between rail and barge rates.

In practice, this approach would call for making an approximate assessment of the value of the quality differences to consumers between the charter service and the discount-promotional service in question, and applying that value as the measure of the rate spread between the two services. The principal elements comprising these differences are readily identifiable and include the advantages ordinarily associated in the public mind with scheduled as against charter service, allowing for the various restrictions applicable to one service or the other. Assigning a value to these differences necessarily involves a subjective type of regulatory determination. What is required is reasonableness, not precision, on the part of the regulator.

The situation is different with regard to competition between charter service offered by the scheduled airlines and charter service offered by the supplementals. Here, the product is much the same in both cases—a seat on a charter flight under stipulated travel restrictions, which vary for different types of charters but are the same for a given type of charter whether carried by a scheduled or a supplemental airline. Differences in equipment may be of competitive significance, but either group has access to the same types of equipment, whether through ownership or leasing. At one time, a charter carried by a major scheduled airline may have had a premium value from the standpoint of consumers, but with the growth of supplemental airlines into major enterprises in their own right —enterprises which are in some cases corporate subsidiaries of large conglomerate firms—there is no service-quality differential requiring a corresponding price-differential to assure competitive equilibrium.

A hybrid situation arises in the case of consolidation of charter and scheduled passengers on scheduled flights, as proposed earlier in this study. Where part of the capacity on a scheduled flight is being used to provide charter service, the question of whether such service should be required to bear a higher price than planeload charter service is open to debate.

From one standpoint, inasmuch as the same travel restrictions—advance booking, deposits, forfeitures, affinity—would apply to both forms of charter service, the rates should be the same for both. From another point of view, charter transportation on a regularly scheduled flight of a route carrier may be viewed as having superior attraction to consumers.

Good arguments can be advanced on behalf of either view. The choice between them can sensibly be based on which one fits better with other regulatory measures which are needed to improve the air transport situation in the North Atlantic.

One solution to what rate difference, if any, would be appropriate is for the matter to hinge upon the conditions of the charter contract. If the contract requires the charter to be carried on a scheduled flight, the superior characteristics of the service in the public mind would justify a premium above the planeload charter rate to counterbalance the difference in customer appeal. If the contract leaves the carrier with the option of providing the charter service either on a planeload basis or on a scheduled flight, the passenger is not assured of the scheduled service and the planeload rate would apply.

Charter Rates

The principles laid out above are the basis for a proper regulatory concept of what constitutes an economically sound system of pricing of scheduled services. But the industry is made up of more than scheduled services. A significant fraction of North Atlantic travel is on charter flights, and the low-price sector of that travel, where scheduled and charter service are in head-on competition with each other, represents about four-fifths of the market. In these circumstances, no regulatory scheme for achieving economic fares can be effective unless it embraces fares for charter as well as scheduled service.

In highly competitive markets in industry generally, supply offerings at the lowest end of the price scale can have a pervasive influence on the price structure of the entire market. The

North Atlantic is no exception. In the low-price segments of the market, where the competitive struggle between scheduled and supplemental airlines is waged, discount-promotional fares and charter prices are closely and dynamically linked. Their effect upon each other is reciprocal. Low charter prices bring low discount-promotional rates and vice versa. Up to a point such competitive price interaction is healthy and serves the interest of the public in getting the most for its money. But it can also be unhealthy and defeat the larger interest of the public in a healthy economic basis for supplying the transportation it needs.

Scheduled and supplemental carriers agree that both charter rates and discount-promotional fares are uneconomically low, and that heavy losses have resulted for both groups. But they differ as to what has caused this uneconomic situation and how to cure it.

The scheduled airlines argue that charter competition "has forced the adoption of uneconomic scheduled fares [with] disastrous profit results of all transatlantic carriers, both scheduled and charter".[22] The supplementals perceive scheduled pricing policies as the root

[22] Comments of Trans World Airlines on International Aviation Policy Review, April 7, 1975, p. 9.

of the evil: "The IATA carriers have been injured because the promotional fares have diluted yields and increased losses . . . [B]elow-cost promotional fares compete unfairly with charter services . . . The supplemental carriers, in order to survive at all, have often been forced to price their services at uneconomic levels".[23]

The same basic principles of sound business practice and sound economics outlined earlier apply to the pricing of an airline's charter services. Fares for the airline as a whole should cover its costs as a whole, including a reasonable return on capital, and fares for individual services should be above incremental costs and no lower than necessary to meet competition. When unrestrained competition in the low-price segments of the North Atlantic travel market drives both discount-promotional and charter prices too low, however, the economic viability of both scheduled and supplemental airlines is undermined. Discount-promotional and charter services account for three-fourths of the total traffic of the scheduled carriers, and charter service accounts for all of the traffic of the supplementals. When the rates of both scheduled and

[23] Comments of National Air Carrier Association on International Aviation Policy Review, April 7, 1975, pp. 14–16.

supplemental airlines in bidding for the low-price travel sector fall far below full costs, operating at meager profits or substantial losses is inevitable for both groups.

While scheduled service is subject to inter-governmental approval of fares established on an industry-wide basis, similar controls are not now applied to charter rates. It is not necessary to resolve the chicken-and-egg question as between excessively low discount-promotional fares and excessively low charter fares to realize that the regulatory task of bringing under control the pressures producing uneconomic prices in the North Atlantic is almost hopelessly burdened so long as a major force affecting the level of charges in the dominant sector of the market remains for all practical purposes outside the scope of effective regulation.

The Civil Aeronautics Board has indicated its belief that discount-promotional fares should be increased. While such an increase is undoubtedly part of the solution required for uneconomic fare levels in the low-price segments of the North Atlantic market, it can not do the job in isolation from an attack upon the charter fares with which they compete for low-price travel business. Raising the level of discount-promotional fares while charter prices went unregulated would simply result in a further shift of traffic from scheduled to charter service, and would worsen rather than improve the financial results of scheduled operations. The answer lies in bringing charter prices under minimum rate regulation.

Minimum rate regulation in any field inevitably raises questions as to the interests of consumers. Many feel that the lower the price of a commodity, the better for the public, and that governments should be more concerned with the economic advantage of consumers than with the well-being of enterprises. In transportation, however, balanced public policy requires not simply the lowest possible rates, but the lowest possible rates consistent with economic soundness.

The principle was cogently set forth a decade ago in a comprehensive staff study of the U.S. Senate Commerce Committee on the subject of National Transportation Policy. While the study deals primarily with surface transportation, the basic concept involved is equally applicable to air transport:

"[D]espite the obvious interest of the user in policies which will encourage the lowest possible rates, a soundly conceived policy for controlling minimum rates in transportation is consistent with the longrun interest of users. Indeed the main justification for law regulating minimum rates is not the protection of producer interests, but rather the maintenance of a sound, diversified transportation system for the benefit of all users."[24]

Regulating minimum charter prices involves administrative complexities, but not of an insuperable nature. Such minimum rates would cover the charter operations of scheduled and supplemental airlines alike, and could be expressed in terms of per-seat-mile or per-plane-mile charges, as determined to be appropriate in the circumstances. These minimum charges could vary with such demand factors as seasonality or direction. Inasmuch as some cost factors, such as terminal expenses, are not distance-related, minimum per-mile charges need not be uniform for point-to-point routes which are substantially different in distance.

While the financial condition of the airlines in the North Atlantic requires the stabilizing influence of a floor on charter rates, it does not justify providing rewards to inefficiency. Accordingly, the basic standard governing a schedule of minimum charges should be the full eco-

[24] "National Transportation Policy", Report of the Committee on Commerce, United States Senate, 87th Congress, 1st Session, Washington, D.C., 1961, p. 417.

nomic cost of the service as performed by an efficient operator, including a return on invested capital.

The Civil Aeronautics Board requires advance filings of charter tariffs. This requirement assures an opportunity for timely review of charter rates and possible suspension of rates deemed unreasonable, but it is no substitute for direct regulation. Effective control of minimum charter rates requires not only advance notice to the Board as to proposed charges, but advance notice from the Board as to the charges which will be considered unreasonable. The filing requirement has not had a significant effect on charter rate levels.

Even the promulgation of specified minimum rates, however, may not be sufficient if the rates are set too low to have any practical effect. This is the situation in the United Kingdom, where control of minimum charter rates has officially been in effect for the past two years. The rates established by the Civil Aviation Authority have not kept up with inflation and have little commercial impact. A similar situation obtains in other countries.

Three years ago an effort was made by the supplemental and the scheduled airlines to develop industry agreement on minimum charter rates in the North Atlantic. That effort failed. Subsequently, the CAB proposed a rule to impose minimum rate regulation on charters originating in the United States. That proposal was dropped.

The lack of controls over charter rates is a serious leak in the regulatory system. Until it is repaired, discount-promotional as well as charter fares will remain depressed below economic levels, and revenues and income sorely needed by scheduled and supplemental airlines alike will continue to be pointlessly sacrificed. A mechanism of regulation tied to the minimum rates needed to support efficient operation would guarantee that the public would pay no more and no less for charter service than it rightfully should bear, and would fortify the airlines, both supplemental and scheduled, with the means of providing low-price service on an economically self-sufficient basis. A new initiative is required to create such a mechanism. The first step is for the industry to make another try at finding common ground. The stakes are high enough, and conditions grave enough, to justify a renewed effort to negotiate differences that formerly may have seemed insurmountable.

Bringing charter rates under control would eliminate a major inconsistency in North Atlantic rate regulation. An industry conference mechanism will be needed to establish industry-wide rates, subject to government review, somewhat along the lines now followed in developing inter-airline agreement on scheduled fares. Scheduled and supplemental carriers would participate in this process. Only the scheduled carriers now participate in IATA conference machinery for establishing discount-promotional fares. To avoid creating another inconsistency, and to insure the needed harmonization between discount-promotional and charter fares, changes in IATA arrangements are called for to give supplemental airlines similar rights in determining the level of discount-promotional fares to those the scheduled airlines would have in determining the level of charter fares.

Some scheduled carriers may well feel that it would be inappropriate for the supplementals to participate in the establishment of rates for services they do not supply. Such a view misses the crucial point. The rationale for bringing charter fares under regulation is that discount-promotional fares and charter rates are closely linked from a competitive standpoint, that the segments of the market to which they appeal account for the lion's share of all North Atlantic air travel, that unrestrained competition in this major part of the market has driven both types of fares down to clearly uneconomic levels, and that this situation can not be cured while charter rates remain outside the ambit of regulation. If scheduled airlines are to have a voice in the establishment of charter rates with which discount-promotional fares must compete, it is equitable that the supplementals be given a corresponding voice in establishing the level of the discount-promotional fares against which charter services compete. Scheduled and supplemental carriers have a strong interest in finding common ground for a set of discount-promotional and charter fares that are equitable to both groups. While their interests are not identical, scheduled and supplemental carriers alike have so much to gain from a flexible and responsible approach to negotiation of economic rates in the low-price travel sector that there is reason for optimism as to the results when both groups of carriers deal with both groups of fares.

Standard of Reasonableness of Profits

Earlier the point was made that the public interest is well served when revenues are adequate to cover total costs of efficient operation, including a reasonable economic profit. It was also stressed that the other side of the coin is that the public has a right to assurance that profits are not excessive. That assurance is not easy to provide in the case of an industry made up of enterprises of different nationality, owing no financial accountability to any supranational body and subscribing to no universally accepted standard of reasonableness of profits. A sufficient showing along this line is nevertheless necessary, particularly where rather far-reaching measures to rationalize capacity and place a floor under rates are being imposed in order to increase the flow of industry revenue and income.

Providing an adequate composite industry picture of profitability should be feasible despite the reluctance of some carriers to disclose financial details of their operations. Some of the data relevant to the required showing are already available. IATA collects various types of financial data on North Atlantic scheduled operations from its member airlines, and publishes such data on an aggregate basis. Regulatory authorities in the United States and the United Kingdom require the submission and publication of pertinent data from their national carriers. What is required is a plausible demonstration that North Atlantic air transport as a whole, and its major segments, the scheduled airlines and the supplemental airlines, are operating within reasonable limits of profit. This may seem a needless showing at present, when industry losses in the North Atlantic amount to hundreds of millions of dollars annually. But public acceptance of needed regulatory changes to turn the situation around will be more readily given if there is some assurance that these changes will not produce excess profits and if there is some credible means of keeping the public informed as to the facts concerning the general level of profitability. The data already published for individual carriers in the U.S. and U.K., amplified to show financial results for North Atlantic operations separately, could serve as a check on the validity of composite industry figures.

As for an acceptable standard of reasonable profitability, the purpose in hand can be served, initially at least, by using the CAB standard of a reasonable return on investment for trunkline passenger service in the United States. That standard is based on the cost of debt and equity capital for United States airlines. Capital costs are lower in the U.S. than elsewhere in the North Atlantic area, and the CAB standard—

now set at an after-tax return of 12 per cent on total invested capital—could therefore be regarded as conservative when applied to the North Atlantic industry.

IV

Conclusion

THE CENTRAL problem with which this study has been concerned is the need to remedy the unhealthy state of air transport in the North Atlantic.

Underlying the entire study has been the recurring set of themes that the chronic ills of air transportation in the North Atlantic are largely due to failure to conform to basic principles of economic efficiency, that the interest of the public as well as of the airlines is impaired when the industry serving this greatest intercontinental air market of all is unable to cover its operating and capital costs, and that economic self-sufficiency can not be attained without fundamental changes in regulatory policies toward capacity and pricing.

The opening chapter dealt with the requisites of a sound regulatory policy for treating the serious economic ills of the industry. It emphasized the importance of meeting the unavoidable political realities of the situation, of blending control and competition in a practical regulatory design, and of accommodating the proper interests of the scheduled and the supplemental segments of the industry and of the general public. It stressed above all the importance of focusing on the right objectives: more efficient use of airline resources and an economic level and structure of fares.

The next two chapters were addressed to the measures needed for fulfilling each of these objectives and doing so in a manner consistent with the requisites of sound regulation. Specific proposals were advanced to achieve improved efficiency by reducing or eliminating surplus flight frequencies in scheduled service, preventing capacity excesses in charter service, and eliminating barriers to the mixing of scheduled and charter passengers on the same flights. With respect to achieving economic fares, principles which should guide regulatory policy with respect to efficient pricing of airline services, including the harmonization of scheduled and charter fares and the need for establishing a floor under charter rates, were set forth. Suitable government and industry mechanisms for achieving the needed changes in capacity and pricing policies were outlined.

The most glaring defect of the system of regulation now governing air transport in the North Atlantic is that it is not geared to the great changes which have transformed the market and the industry over the past ten to fifteen years. Bilateral Bermuda-type clauses[1] for post-facto intergovernmental consultations concerning scheduled capacity may have been adequate to deal with problems of capacity excess in the North Atlantic in an era when such problems arose only occasionally and basically affected only the traffic between the two signatory countries, and when non-scheduled service was of little consequence. But such arrangements can not suffice to meet the chronic problems of surplus capacity which characterize the North Atlantic today when the number of competing

[1] The United States–United Kingdom bilateral air agreement signed in Bermuda in 1946 declared as a primary objective "the provision of capacity adequate to the traffic demands". The clause is generally regarded as standing for the principle of meeting the problems of excess capacity not by pre-determination of the two signatories to an air bilateral but by intergovernmental consultation and negotiation after a specific excess develops and reaches serious proportions.

airlines has risen dramatically, when the frequency of flights is perceived by all airlines to have a crucial effect upon market position, when the advent of the jumbo jet has multiplied, many times over, the seat supply available on each flight, and when charter service accounts for one-fourth of the total passenger traffic and competitively interacts with scheduled service. By the same token, lack of industry conference or intergovernmental machinery to deal with capacity problems on a multilateral basis may once have been of little importance, but in the jet age, with the great competitive overlap of country-to-country routings across much of the North Atlantic market, the absence of such machinery is sorely felt.

In the days when airplanes were smaller and less expensive and fuel and labor costs were lower, the enforced segregation of scheduled and charter passengers on separate flights was only a minor extravagance. Today the needless waste of seating capacity on scheduled flights is an exuberant luxury neither the industry nor the public can afford.

Along similar lines, limiting industry rate agreements to fares for scheduled service has become anachronistic when three-fourths of the passengers carried on scheduled flights move on low-fare discount and promotional service which must compete with charter fares that are virtually unregulated. Charter travel and discount-promotional travel are competitive alternatives. Minimum rate regulation is considered important enough to justify its use in determining discount-promotional fares. But no corresponding approach is employed in determining charter fares. The result is an anomaly that can not help but undermine the fare structure of both discount-promotional and charter services which together account for four-fifths of the total North Atlantic traffic.

The economic problems of air transport in the North Atlantic arise from forces which cut across the entire market and affect all segments of the industry. Only an all-encompassing regulatory approach can cope with such problems. Capacity and price, as every economist knows, are in continual interaction with each other, and a total attack upon the economic ills of the industry must therefore comprehend both.

Capacity, in turn, can not be only partially controlled. Controlling scheduled capacity would save resources and reduce costs but it cannot be effective if charter capacity, with which it competes, is permitted to proliferate without restraint. On the other hand, controlling scheduled capacity requires measures to assure that the capacity released is not used in a way that contributes to capacity excess in charter service. Regulation permitting the consolidation of scheduled and charter services on scheduled flights in order to put otherwise wasted capacity to efficient use demands concomitant regulation to make sure that the charter market is not swamped by this added source of charter capacity. Regardless of where the circle begins, it must be followed completely around the problems it seeks to cure.

Similarly with respect to price, remedial measures, to be effective, must deal with the whole syndrome of problems which need attention. Rules of efficient pricing call for the scheduled airlines to respond to consumer demand and to competitive charter service by offering discount-promotional fares at any margin above incremental cost, but the requirements of healthy competition necessitate a further rule that such fares shall be no lower than necessary to meet the charter competition at a point of equilibrium. An analogous differential may well be in order between fares for charter passengers when carried on scheduled flights and fares for charter passengers moving on regular charter flights. As for the inconsistency which now prevails with regard to regulation of rates for scheduled and charter services, it would be no less valid to control charter fares and ignore discount-promotional fares than to do the reverse, as in the present regulatory scheme. So long as low-price scheduled and charter services are in direct competition, both types of fares must be controlled, and in a way that gives supplemental as well as scheduled carriers a voice in the establishment of both.

Present regulatory policies do not come to grips with the real, basic causes of the economic plight of the industry. The choice in the North Atlantic is not between regulation or no regulation. For reasons discussed elsewhere in this study, abandonment of regulation there, or in international air transport generally, is politically out of the question. The only choice is between effective and ineffective regulation.

Regulatory policy is peculiarly the prerogative of governments rather than of airlines. Governments have the ultimate authority as well as the ultimate responsibility of leadership. But the airlines also have an unmistakable obligation to discern, initiate, and press for changes in regulatory policy which can revitalize North Atlantic air transportation in a manner which serves the public and is beneficial to both scheduled and supplemental sectors of the industry.

The North Atlantic system lies at the crucial center of world air transport. Almost one-third of all international air travel moves on that system. The economic ills to which international air transport is particularly susceptible take their most virulent form in the North Atlantic. But many of the same debilitating factors which have made the North Atlantic an economic disaster area are already at work in other major areas. The measures proposed in this study can serve to restore the sick North Atlantic system to economic vitality, and in doing so can help to prevent the repetition of the North Atlantic experience elsewhere.

Appendix

TABLE 1
NORTH ATLANTIC PASSENGER TRAFFIC
By Air and Sea
1955–1975
(Thousands of Passengers)

YEAR	TOTAL	AIR PASSENGERS	SEA PASSENGERS	AIR PASSENGERS AS PERCENT OF TOTAL
1955	1,682	720	962	42.8%
56	1,881	870	1,011	46.3
57	2,087	1,060	1,027	50.8
58	2,304	1,340	964	58.2
59	2,481	1,600	881	64.5
1960	2,879	2,000	879	69.5
61	3,045	2,260	785	74.2
62	3,510	2,690	820	76.6
63	3,768	2,958	810	78.5
64	4,473	3,758	715	84.0
1965	5,066	4,417	649	87.2
66	5,753	5,150	603	89.5
67	6,684	6,180	504	92.5
68	7,045	6,671	374	94.7
69	8,709	8,371	338	96.1
1970	10,216	9,964	252	97.5
71	11,257	11,040	217	98.1
72	13,217	13,102	115	99.1
73	14,178	14,085	93	99.3
74	12,879	12,823	56	99.6
1975	12,450	12,400	50[a]	99.6

[a] Estimated.

SOURCE: *International Air Transport Association. (Includes estimates of non-IATA traffic) Data on sea passengers are collected by IATA from maritime companies.*

TABLE 2

NORTH ATLANTIC AIR PASSENGER TRAFFIC

By Type of Carrier, Service, and Fare

1963–1975

(Thousands of Passengers)

YEAR	(1) TOTAL NORTH ATLANTIC TRAFFIC (2) + (7)	(2) TOTAL (3) + (6)	(3) TOTAL, ALL FARES	(4) SCHEDULED SERVICE[1] DISCOUNT-PROMOTIONAL FARES	(5) FULL FARES	(6) CHARTER SERVICE	(7) SUPPLEMENTAL CARRIERS (CHARTER SERVICE)[2]	(8) TOTAL CHARTER SERVICE (6) + (7)
			NUMBER OF PASSENGERS (THOUSANDS)					
1963	2,958	2,903	2,489	871	1,618	414	55	469
64	3,758	3,646	3,164	1,259	1,905	482	112	594
65	4,417	4,219	3,739	1,475	2,264	480	198	678
66	5,150	4,847	4,344	1,975	2,371	503	303	806
1967	6,180	5,670	5,153	2,475	2,678	517	510	1,027
68	6,671	5,918	5,423	2,773	2,650	495	753	1,248
69	8,371	6,960	6,180	3,513	2,667	780	1,411	2,191
70	9,964	8,280	7,463	5,123	2,340	817	1,684	2,501
1971	11,040	8,859	7,800	5,544	2,256	1,059	2,181	3,240
72	13,102	11,126	9,797	7,674	2,123	1,329	1,976	3,305
73	14,085	12,000	10,329	8,011	2,318	1,671	2,085	3,756
74	12,823	10,783	9,640	6,968	2,672	1,143	2,040	3,183
1975	12,400	10,350	9,082	6,494	2,588	1,268	2,050	3,318

PERCENT DISTRIBUTION[3]

1963	100.0%	98.1%	84.1%	29.4%	54.7%	14.0%	1.9%	15.9%
64	100.0	97.0	84.2	33.5	50.7	12.8	3.0	15.8
65	100.0	95.5	84.7	33.4	51.3	10.9	4.5	15.3
66	100.0	94.1	84.3	38.3	46.0	9.8	5.9	15.7
1967	100.0	91.7	83.4	40.0	43.3	8.4	8.3	16.6
68	100.0	88.7	81.3	41.6	39.7	7.4	11.3	18.7
69	100.0	83.1	73.8	42.0	31.9	9.3	16.9	26.2
70	100.0	83.1	74.9	51.4	23.5	8.2	16.9	25.1
1971	100.0	80.2	70.7	50.2	20.4	9.6	19.8	29.3
72	100.0	84.9	74.8	58.6	16.2	10.1	15.1	25.2
73	100.0	85.2	73.3	56.9	16.5	11.9	14.8	26.7
74	100.0	84.1	75.2	54.3	20.8	8.9	15.9	24.8
1975	100.0	83.5	73.2	52.4	20.9	10.2	16.5	26.8

[1] Includes traffic of non-IATA scheduled carriers.
[2] Includes traffic of certain charter affiliates of scheduled airlines; in 1974 these affiliates accounted for 4 percent of total charter traffic.
[3] Because of rounding, totals will not necessarily add across.
SOURCE: *International Air Transport Association traffic statistics. (Includes estimates of non-IATA traffic.)*

TABLE 3
NORTH ATLANTIC AIR PASSENGER TRAFFIC
By Type of Fare
1963–1975
(Thousands of Passengers)

YEAR	TOTAL NORTH ATLANTIC TRAFFIC	FULL-FARE TRAFFIC			LOW-FARE TRAFFIC		
		TOTAL	FIRST CLASS	NORMAL ECONOMY	TOTAL	DISCOUNT-PROMOTIONAL[1]	CHARTER
		NUMBER OF PASSENGERS (THOUSANDS)					
1963	2,958	1,618	208	1,410	1,340	871	469
64	3,758	1,905	245	1,660	1,853	1,259	594
65	4,417	2,264	289	1,975	2,153	1,475	678
66	5,150	2,371	344	2,027	2,779	1,973	806
1967	6,180	2,678	379	2,299	3,502	2,475	1,027
68	6,671	2,650	384	2,266	4,021	2,773	1,248
69	8,371	2,667	484	2,183	5,704	3,513	2,191
70	9,964	2,340	475	1,865	7,624	5,123	2,501
1971	11,040	2,256	448	1,808	8,784	5,544	3,240
72	13,102	2,123	455	1,668	10,979	7,674	3,305
73	14,085	2,318	481	1,837	11,767	8,011	3,756
74	12,823	2,672	500	2,172	10,151	6,968	3,183
1975	12,400	2,588	471	2,117	9,812	6,494	3,318

PERCENT DISTRIBUTION[2]

1963	100.0%	54.7%	7.0%	47.7%	45.3%	29.4%	15.9%
64	100.0	50.7	6.5	44.2	49.3	33.5	15.8
65	100.0	51.3	6.5	44.7	48.7	33.4	15.3
66	100.0	46.0	6.7	39.4	54.0	38.3	15.7
1967	100.0	43.3	6.1	37.2	56.7	40.0	16.6
68	100.0	39.7	5.8	34.0	60.3	41.6	18.7
69	100.0	31.9	5.8	26.1	68.1	42.0	26.2
70	100.0	23.5	4.8	18.7	76.5	51.4	25.1
1971	100.0	20.4	4.1	16.4	79.6	50.2	29.3
72	100.0	16.2	3.5	12.7	83.8	58.6	25.2
73	100.0	16.5	3.4	13.0	83.5	56.9	26.6
74	100.0	20.8	3.9	16.9	79.2	54.3	24.8
1975	100.0	20.9	3.8	17.1	79.1	52.4	26.8

[1] Includes all IATA scheduled traffic other than full-fare and all non-IATA scheduled traffic.
[2] Because of rounding, totals will not necessarily add across.
SOURCE: *International Air Transport Association traffic statistics. (Includes estimates of non-IATA traffic.)*